All the world's a stage.

MW00804441

Journey
to the
Stage

Compiled and Presented by
Women's Prosperity Network

Parker House Publishing
www.ParkerHouseBooks.com

©2015 Women's Prosperity Network, Inc.
All rights reserved.
No part of this book may be reproduced by mechanical, photographic, or electronic process, or in the form of recording, nor may it be stored in a retrieval system, transmitted or otherwise be copied for public use or private use – other than "fair use" as brief quotations embodied in articles and reviews, without prior written permission of the publisher and/or authors.

This book is designed to provide information and inspiration to our readers. It is sold with the understanding that the publisher and the authors are not engaged in the rendering of psychological, legal, accounting or other professional advice. The content is the sole expression and opinion of the authors and not necessarily of the publisher. No warranties or guaranties are expressed or implied by the publisher's choice to include any of the content in this book. Neither the publisher nor the authors shall be liable for any physical, psychological, emotional, financial, or commercial damages, including but not limited to special, incidental, consequential or other damages. Our views and rights are the same: You are responsible for your own choices, actions and results.
Book design: Candi Parker
Editing: Judee Light

Published by ParkerHouseBooks.com

First Printing July 2015

This book is available at quantity discounts for bulk purchases and for branding by businesses and organizations. For further information or to learn more about Women's Prosperity Network, contact
Team@WomensProsperityNetwork.com
or call (800) 928-6928.

Contributing Authors

Allison Ronis
Ana Atibet
Beverly Sorrells
Carla Hutchinson
Cat Wagman
Cynthia Chevrestt
Deborah Brown
Gail Dixon
Georgianna Rivera
Ginny Milu
Jamie Gilleland
Janis David
Jenny Battig
Johnny Regan
Kathy Pendleton
Licia Berry
Linda Allred
Linda DeMarco
Martin Butler
Melanie Berry
Paulina Lopez
Revella Hadley
Sandra Hanesworth
Stephanie Pimental
Varsha Bhongade
Vicki Ibaugh
Yvonne Green

Introduction

The inspiration for this book came about at the end of a 3-day intensive training for people who had chosen to step up and step onto the world's stage in a bigger way, that is, by becoming certified professional speakers.

They were ordinary people, just like you and like us, who decided to accept this extraordinary challenge and step out of their comfort zones and into the spotlight. They were all fueled by passion and commitment, yet we could recognize different motivating factors that caused them to accept the challenge and attend the training:

Some wanted to overcome a fear that had crippled them in the past.

Some sought to become more polished and effective in their presentations.

Some were eager to become more powerful influencers to inspire the audience to take action.

While the initial motivating factors differed, the common thread for every individual in this class (and in all the classes we've held before this), is that every person who accepts this challenge is driven by a deep desire to increase their reach and their impact to make a difference in the lives of others.

It was that deep desire to make a difference in the lives of others that spurred the inspiration for this book so that you, the reader, would discover solutions, ideas and opportunities to experience your place on the world's stage in a more meaningful and joyful way.

This book includes contributions from long-time speakers, first time speakers and accidental speakers. Every story is delivered in a heartfelt, authentic fashion where the authors' passion to add value, be of service and make a contribution to the world causes them to continuously step up and step out to share their message.

Whether you're claiming your place on the stage in your own corner of the world or you're eager to reach all four corners of the world, this book will ignite your passion, inspire creativity and move you to action.

Enjoy Your Journey to the Stage!

Nancy, Trish & Susan
Founders, Women's Prosperity Network

About Women's Prosperity Network

Nancy Matthews, Trish Carr and Susan Wiener are three sisters (yes, real sisters with the same mother and the same father!) They founded Women's Prosperity Network in 2008 fueled by their passion and deep desire for women to recognize and embrace their own greatness and to honor the greatness in each other. They encourage and empower women to "Be Real, Get Real & Achieve Real Results" through ongoing mastermind sessions, workshops and seminars.

Since 2008 they have served over 10,000 women and men through a continuing community of support providing inspiration, education and a network of dynamic connections.

Their vision is a global community of impassioned, determined women, committed to supporting each other's pursuit of excellence and significantly impacting our world.

To learn more about Women's Prosperity Network (yes, men are invited too!), go to:

WomensProsperityNetwork.com
Email: Team@WomensProsperityNetwork
Phone: (800) 928-6928

Table of Contents

Deborah Brown

works with clients to define and design their lives to incorporate their personal as well as professional aspirations. As a senior ranking consultant in the IT industry for 14 years, Deborah knows first-hand how difficult it can be to attain work-life balance and what happens to your spirit when you give all you have to the job. Her personal desire for fulfillment and witnessing so many other professionals experiencing similar challenges were the impetus and inspiration for entering the coaching profession and creating her company, Optimal Leap, Inc. Her greatest expertise and passion revolve around relating to people and she combines her knowledge and experience to deliver the best results to her clients.

You can connect with Deborah at:
Deborah@OptimalLeap.com
www.OptimalLeap.com

An Unexpected Journey

Deborah Brown

As a somewhat shy girl growing up, the last thing I would have ever dreamed or thought of was a future or career that involved speaking on stage – it was the furthest thing from my mind. My exposure to any level of public speaking came from mandatory academic presentations in high school and college - excruciating events that I dreaded - and in my professional career where, as a senior project manager, leading meetings with my teams and doing presentations for executive client teams were part of the job description.

While the breadth of my speaking in the past primarily involved relaying information about technical matters such as studies and status updates, what I do today is vastly different. Today, my experience of public speaking takes the form of conveying personal stories of my journey and occurs in front of an audience of strangers who, after getting personal with them, I can then call new friends.

To give a bit of insight, my personal story speaks of my own transition and transformation at the professional level. I was working for years in a field and career that, although great by everyone else's standards including mine at one time, lacked the level of fulfillment that I was seeking at that particular stage of my life. It did not tap into my greatest talents, passion, and skills to the degree that I wanted. For 14 years, I was consulting in the IT field and moved through the ranks to senior management. While the experience was thrilling at first, in the latter years as I began to move on to different phases of my life, it no longer fully served me. I should have had nothing to complain about - it was a *great opportunity* - a *great* salary, *great* people to work with, *great* work that offered the novelty and challenges that I commonly sought, *great* travel and associated perks, *great* clients – many of the top organizations, but at the heart of it all, it just was no longer *great* for me.

Throughout my years in a senior role, the aspect of the work that I most enjoyed was training, mentoring and coaching my teams, and I yearned for more of that on a deeper level. That desire that I could not ignore led me to where I am and who I am today. Today, I am a professional coach and I work with people who have a similar awareness that some aspect of their life is not entirely of their own choosing, and I support them in defining that and stepping into one that is. I work with individuals who want to be more, do more and have more and are ready to claim it!

My passion to serve people truly drove me to the stage. My mindset around speaking changed with advice that was given to me. A mentor of mine once told me that I am doing my potential clients - the people who are waiting to benefit from the work I do, the people who could be touched by my message, the people whose quality of life could be improved through my work - a disservice by not showing up and making myself available to a larger audience pool. As much as the more personal touch and connecting with people on a one-on-one basis is my preferred mode of operation, it was clear to me that that approach would not serve the greater cause and my purpose.

My first formal introduction to the world of speaking came with my first speaker's training with Les Brown. I watched my own transformation from a nervous basket case standing on a stage amongst people who clearly had been on this track for years or were naturally gifted. I transformed from the person who needed a script as her crutch to one who spoke from the heart. This was the first time that I was asked to get personal, and I do have to admit that it was a bit challenging. That experience was, of course, not enough to turn me into a great speaker but planted the seed that it was possible, which coincidentally is one of Les Brown's key messages.

My competence in speaking improved significantly with that training, but my comfort level before an audience left a lot to be desired. That was the case until a coach of mine reminded me that, like so many things in life, what you focus on expands and is what becomes most important. Speaking was no different. If the focus was on me, my performance and dealing with my own hang-ups and nervousness around speaking, then my self-consciousness was counter-productive and made my delivery less effective. When the focus was on the message being delivered, the knowledge and information being shared and the possibility that someone in the audience could benefit, the experience and my outlook changed dramatically. I am reminded of the spiritual quote, "Less of me, more of Thee." When we put ourselves in the position of service – service to the audience - and take the ego out of it, there leaves only room for love and true authenticity to shine.

Now I actively seek opportunities to speak, to reach people, because the chance that someone can find comfort in knowing that they are not alone in their own situation, that someone can relate and is able to support them on their journey, excites me. Realizing my purpose has fueled my desire to connect with people who have experienced or are experiencing similar challenges and situations. Without fail, each time I speak, I am met by someone at the end who says that that is or was their story... and I am reminded of why I do it and will continue to do it.

The experience has truly been one of my own personal growth. My company's name is Optimal Leap which means "Leap to Your Best Self" and I often speak about the need for each of us to raise our own bar. Conquering my fear around speaking, getting out of my comfort zone and making an impact in a whole new way was my opportunity to do just that. It was my opportunity to strip myself of the *shy* label that I had given myself for years.

As much as I know there are benefits for the audience, I have come to appreciate the gems that are available for me in this work as well. Some of these include the fact that I have the privilege of connecting with a variety of people with whom I possibly would not have otherwise had the opportunity to connect. Telling my story gives people an opening and, in many cases, permission to express themselves, release and, in some cases, admit feelings that they have stuffed down or denied. It is encouraging to see that this work can lead to someone's self-awareness and a safe place for self-expression.

Then lastly is the gift of authenticity and vulnerability. To stand in front of an audience and reveal the experiences and parts of me that are less than perfect and give an audience a front-row view to my deepest emotions is liberating. It serves as a reconfirmation of sorts that creating the life you love is possible and that anyone in the audience can do it if I could do it. The possibility of playing a role in improving someone's perspective of the quality of their life, as I have seen time and time again with my clients, is the power that fuels my conviction to continue sharing the message.

It has often been said that speakers turn their mess into their message and their tests into their testimony. Speaking provides a great outlet for anyone with a desire to help, influence or impact others. Each of us has had a unique set of experiences from which we have learned and grown. That puts us in the ideal position to support someone who is experiencing something similar. Sometimes, the challenge may not even be the same but what resonates with the audience is the human emotion and experience behind it that can be transferred to a different situation they are encountering. Sometimes it only takes the attitude, the outlook, and the triumph in your story to inspire, elevate a person's level of thinking, and give them new hope and determination.

Gail Dixon

is a national Speaker, Author, Coach, and Consultant and President of *Mastering Authentic Change*. She has been recognized nationally and in her own community as a leader in women's issues, non-profit organizational development, addiction services and change management. As an expert in change facilitation for individuals and organizations, Gail uses her own success as a catalyst to move others through some of life's most difficult moments. Her expert communication skills lead others past the fear and frustration of the change process so that they attain their goals, create lasting results and achieve authentic change.

Contact Gail at:
(850) 212-3451
gail@MasteringAuthenticChange.com
www.MasteringAuthenticChange.com

The Heart's Voice

Gail Dixon

For as long as I can remember, I have been fascinated with the power of words. My mother told me that I started talking at nine months old and that I didn't know when to stop. She was right – my otherwise good report cards often carried a bad mark for "talking in class." It didn't take much imagination to figure out that, when people referred to me and my sisters, it would be, "Lori is the singer, Cheryl is the dancer and Gail is the talker."

I became a creative dramatics student in kindergarten. Throughout my elementary and high school years, there was a series of plays, speech contests and debates to showcase my talent. Those were times when I was expected to use my voice and my love of words. It felt good. There were other times when it didn't feel so good – when I was shushed or silenced. My voice carries well and sometimes I spoke too loudly for others' comfort. My mind works quickly and sometimes I spoke too freely or frankly. Still, by and large, I liked living out loud.

Over time, though, I began to avoid the spotlight and focus more on the behind-the-scenes work. I can't pinpoint the moment exactly, but I developed a sense that the public platform was not where I should be standing.

Along with that move to the sidelines, my voice changed, although I didn't know it at the time. If I had been a boy, perhaps it would have been more apparent because you (and I) would have heard it when my voice cracked and then moved to the lower register. But the clues for me were much more subtle, and I missed seeing them for what they were at the time. If you'd asked me then, I wouldn't have said that my voice changed. I'd have said that I grew up and became a professional.

That professional self was still in love with words. I became a speech and French teacher and a student of communication. The wonderful nuances of the French language sent me searching for similar gems in English. When I found those gems, they came in multiple syllables and I used every one of them! My circle of friends and colleagues sometimes welcomed it and sometimes winced when I relied on my extensive vocabulary to make a point. Often as not, my wording was a ten-pound rock in a five-pound sack – pretty, but probably twice as much as necessary.

Spending some years as a counselor, I became more focused on listening than on speaking. When I did speak, it was to reflect my clients' words, speaking their own truths back to them so that they could hear them more fully. Even when I used my own words, it was in the service of expressing the client's truth, rather than my own. I suspect that it was in this counseling role that my voice change became complete. I became very fluent in speaking from my head, rather than from my heart – especially in public.

Don't get me wrong. I still shared my emotions with friends and family. But even then, I probably spoke more in the voice of understanding than in the voice of feeling. In fact, I could squeeze the feeling right out of something by processing it to death. It worked for me, but not always for the other person, who often got lost along the way in the midst of all those multi-syllable words.

In the career world, for more than 20 years after I closed my counseling practice, I spoke almost entirely in that voice of the head. As a trainer, group facilitator and curriculum writer, my job was to be a translator of knowledge so that people could put it into practice. It was a job tailor-made for a foreign language major! Translating the words of academics and researchers into language that made sense for practitioners was meaningful work and I did it well.

In my grant writing work with non-profit organizations, I became quite the expert at making the connection between the funder's mission and the agency's work – after all, it was just a matter of how things were said. More than ten million dollars in grants and contracts over the years is evidence that speaking from the head worked well for my clients and employers. And, for a time, it worked well for me, too. I appreciated the good salary, solid benefits and consistent consulting opportunities. I enjoyed the feeling of accomplishment and the sense of making a contribution.

To be honest, I also enjoyed the safety and security of speaking from behind the curtain, rather than in front of it. People knew that I was there, but I did not have to stand in the glare of the spotlight – or its scrutiny. It was much more comfortable for me to do most of my work with words in writing, rather than in speaking. My "head voice" was much better suited for the formality (and distance) of the written word. I might have gone on like this for several more years, but the greater wisdom of the Universe had other ideas!

At a retreat for women about three years ago, I answered one of those fill-in-the-blank self-awareness exercises and life has not been the same since. The question was simple, but the answer has been complicated. I surprised myself with my answer:

I am...The Heart's Voice.

No titles, credentials, or roles were written into that space. "The Heart's Voice?" What in the world is that? What does it mean? What do I do as The Heart's Voice? That three-word answer made me reflect on three decades of using words to make a living and led me to the conclusion that I had been speaking in a less-than-fully-authentic voice. To be sure, the intellectual "head voice" I had been using was truthful, accurate, and even meaningful. It worked well for me and for many others. So -- what was the problem?

The problem was that the head's voice is the changed voice, the one that I began to use when I moved from the stage to the sidelines. The *real voice*, the one I came into this life with, and the one I will be speaking with until I leave this world, is *The Heart's Voice.*

It was a bit of a frightening revelation, because it means more than just a change of perspective or tone. It is a subtle but profound difference in the way I show up in the world. I can speak *from* the head's voice, or *with* the head's voice, but I have to speak *as* The Heart's Voice. It has to be *who I am, not just what I say!* And that means I have to move out of the sidelines and back to the stage. The Heart's Voice can't speak from behind the curtain after all. To *speak* authentically with heart, *as* Heart, I need to be willing to:

Be *seen* authentically with all my flaws, all my fears and my foibles, and

Be *seen* authentically with all of my passion, my purpose and my power!

I am making that move back to my authentic self by taking to the stage and the page speaking as my Heart's Voice, when I share the process of *Mastering Authentic Change.* It has taken me the last three years of thinking it through, planning and working up the courage, and I am ready to embrace the truth of that statement:

I am The Heart's Voice!

Ginny Milu

was born in Chicago, Illinois, into a family of eight. Her family relocated to Ocala, Florida, in 1973, and was transferred to Hialeah, Florida, in 1981. She married Gregg Milu in 2003 and has five children and one grandchild: Heather, Melanie, Justin, Cara, Gregory and Landon. Ginny is a Nutritional Wellness Counselor who has worked from home at Health Rebalancing with Isagenix® (Independent Associate) since January 2014. She was previously a Manager of Delta Laboratories (beginning 1977). She is currently certified as a Specialist in Fitness Nutrition (ISSA) and a Certified Public Speaker (WPN), and holds a Florida Real Estate License.

Contact information:
(954) 290-1860
healthrebalancing@gmail.com
www.healthrebalancing.com
www.ginnymilu.com
www.facebook.com/healthrebalancing

Journey from Fearful to Fearless

Ginny Milu

The first time I remember being on "stage" was in Kindergarten. It was my birthday and everyone was to draw a picture of ME. I was so happy sitting in front of the room having the attention of all my classmates while they worked on their drawings. When the teacher collected their work, we were looking at them together. There was this one boy that drew me naked. Not only that, I looked like him, anatomically! Surely, I never saw what a boy looked like at age five, but knew my body didn't look like that! Completely crushed, I cried all the way home to tell mom.

There were a few other times being the center of attention didn't feel comfortable. Playing the guitar for my parents' friends, after just a few lessons in fourth grade, was one of them. They chose *Malaguena*, a very long song that I had just received from my music teacher. Blushing the whole time and fumbling with the guitar and music sheets was not pleasant, but my audience very attentive. Eighth grade drama class was another uncomfortable time. I was chosen for the school play as the milkman in *Fiddler on the Roof*. I was happy about only having two lines, but not thrilled to be playing a boy. With my long hair stuffed into a baseball cap and being flat-chested, I understand why I got the part. I didn't feel like myself at all, but that's acting! Then in ninth grade modern dance class, I created a routine to the song *Bridge over Troubled Water*. I had not practiced the "whole" song and I was just moving to the music, pretending the routine was planned. Very embarrassed, I wished my classmates and teacher would just fall asleep and *stop watching me!* I was also honored with the privilege to do a reading in church at my brother's wedding. My voice trembled the whole time and I felt like I ruined the service.

As a middle child of eight, I was fairly quiet, never as outgoing or as fun as my older sister. Actually I was considered the cry baby of the family. My older sister commanded attention just walking into the room! I always looked up to her and desired to be more like that.

I didn't really start coming out of my shell until after I started working in 1977. Later as a single mother, I was lucky I had secured an office job at a local paint manufacturer. My confidence and position grew with this company, and for 37 years, this was my career. I did try to leave three times. Instead of moving back to Chicago from Central Florida, I moved south to Miami. I thought about leaving after I attained my Insurance License and considered leaving again when I got my Real Estate License. Life situations, along with the company's promises and security, kept me there.

As a child, I told adults, "I want to help people when I grow up." I just wasn't sure how. Although, I always thought I would attend college after high school, figure it out, and possibly become a nurse or social worker. I went back to college briefly after I married and divorced for a second time having two more children.

While floating from one thing to the next, trying to find myself and my purpose, I met my third husband and love of my life, Gregg, in 1996 and got a glimpse of a great future.

We knew we were meant for each other and felt compelled to stay healthy and active for the long haul, so I entered the world of nutrition and natural healing. Gregg and I studied supplements, learned to meditate, and enjoyed yoga and Qigong. Together we researched what processed foods, GMO's, artificial sweeteners and sugar did to our bodies. Then we found the best cooking oils and spices, and changed our eating habits.

At the time, Gregg and I were looking for a natural healer, and one of my sisters heard about a doctor that her client in the Bahamas visited monthly, Dr. Corey Cameron. She is a chiropractor by degree but practices very different, non-force techniques. One technique is called Contact Reflex Analysis, a method of assessing the body's nutritional and structural deficiencies. She has been our "primary" healthcare practitioner ever since.

In 2006, after four years of seeing Dr. Corey, she introduced us to a nutritional cleansing and replenishing system called Isagenix®. This health system detoxifies the body on a cellular level, builds muscle and rejuvenates it with optimal nutrition. It's kind of like changing the oil in your car! She witnessed amazing results in her clients and after using the products ourselves, we were hooked!

Still searching for my purpose, in 2011, I looked into a school to get certified in Complementary and Alternative Medicine and discussed this with Dr. Corey. I thought that some modality of the training would be what I was looking for, even though going to school part time for three years and the cost of tuition would be somewhat of a challenge. Dr. Corey said I could "serve others" in the field of nutrition with Isagenix® and pointed out that I would not have to worry about seeking employment when I was finished.

So, this exit strategy existed for five years, but I didn't see it! My journey towards better health gave me the opportunity to create a life of serving others, using something I truly believe in. I even have a chance to continue making money after retiring and creating residual income.

After working part time for three years as an Independent Associate with Isagenix®, I took advantage of the opportunity to change lives full time! I resigned from my job in January 2014 to share the gift of health with everyone. The paint company did offer me a salary increase to stay, but it wasn't about money anymore. Soon to be 56, I still didn't feel secure or feel that I had made a difference in this world.

This past year has been quite a voyage in my personal growth. I fill my days networking, sharing my mission to educate and empower others, impacting their health and that of their families, watching them transform both physically and financially. What separates me from other nutritional wellness counselors is that I am certified as a Specialist in Fitness Nutrition. This means I have the education and expertise to guide my clients' meal plans that are used along with this program and throughout life.

One major stumbling block paralyzed me. SPEAKING IN PUBLIC! I found myself petrified to get up and say who I was and what I did even though sometimes it was only for 30 seconds. The heat rising to my face and butterflies in my belly started immediately. I had to do something quickly to overcome this fear. I decided to hire a speaking coach, Trish

Carr of Women's Prosperity Network. She helped me tremendously, reviewing the course of my life so events easily came to mind when connecting with others. We prepared my 30-second, 1-minute and 5-minute speeches. I was determined now that I could do this!

Then a time came when, as a sponsor of an event, I was given the opportunity to speak for 5 minutes to a group of 40. Here was a chance to share my passion with many, instead of just one on one! I knew it was important to take an opportunity like this when given.

With my speech prepared, I practiced over and over, in front of the mirror, while driving, and even videotaped it on my cell phone. I didn't want it to sound like I memorized it (even though I did), or for me to look too stiff when presenting (which I did). It needed to sound like it came from my heart, which it does, since I wrote it. So the date was getting closer, and I was feeling nauseous. I had to do something else. For $250 I was hypnotized prior to the event. This really seemed to boost my confidence. I didn't have the anxiety, nausea or fear I was expecting. Well, about three minutes into my speech, I blurted out "I am so nervous" but amazingly picked right up where I left off!

Obviously, the three one-hour coaching sessions and hypnosis were not enough to fix me! My commitment to share my story, my passion, the business opportunity and nutrition solutions were stronger than my fear of public speaking! Something had to make me overcome that childhood fear of being in the front of the room with all eyes on me. I decided to invest in myself again and signed up for three full days of Speaker's Boot Camp. I became a Certified Public Speaker that weekend! That has propelled me to gain more confidence and conviction in sharing my journey to better health.

Gaining comfort speaking in public opens so many doors. I now more confidently ask to speak about nutrition and the effects of toxins in the body. I speak at small businesses to their employees over lunch, to healthcare practitioners and their patients, to parent groups in schools, and at home parties. I have become a confident leader for my Isagenix® team. The opportunities and benefits are endless!

To grow, get out of your comfort zone and go from FEARFUL to FEARLESS!

"Within each of us there is a visionary. The 'guts' comes from having a team to support, guide and encourage you."
~ Nancy Matthews, "The Visionary with Guts"

Vicki Ibaugh

is on a mission to teach how making a shift in habits can lead to lifelong health and wellness. She is a nurse practitioner and certified health coach. She is the founder and owner of Personalized Health Coaching. After a lifelong journey to fight shyness and find her power and ability, she is now ready to punch fear right in the face. Years of speaking have helped her gain confidence and training to become a certified public speaker that resulted in her finally being ready to step up, step out, and share her message.

Contact Vicki at:
(407) 442-6240
vickie@personalizedhealthcoaching.com
www.personalizedhealthcoaching.com

Shy Girl Discovers Her Power and Her Voice: The Day I Punched Fear Right in the Face

Vicki Ibaugh

When all else fails – panic and CRY!?

If you grew up shy and are reading this book, know that I was once just like you. I might have been even worse. When the teacher started calling on kids to read in class, I would avoid eye contact. I would try to hide and, when she got to my name, I would panic and then I would start to cry. That was my standard response to stress. I would panic and then cry. That pretty much was how all of elementary school went. Except for one glimmer of light – show-and-tell day. For some reason I LOVED to do magic tricks and would willingly stand in line to show my latest trick to the group. It was the first ray of hope that maybe, just maybe, I could be in front of a group and not panic or cry.

Over time, things did improve, but I never really shook that fear of standing in front of a group and opening my mouth. My voice would shake and I would often end up reading from note cards and avoid eye contact just to get through it. My future as an orator was still looking pretty unlikely.

Yet I knew I had important things to say and to share. A little part of me deep down wanted to be able to stand in front of that group and have the words pour out of my mouth like they sounded in my head and the way I practiced in the mirror. In those moments, I always sounded great. Well composed, thoughtful, and insightful. Unfortunately when I opened my mouth in front of a group, the words sounded uncertain and unsure. Thankfully I had at least overcome my "panic turned into tears" issues.

OH, NO! The required Speech class!

Then, like many college students, I had to take the dreaded speech class. It was mandatory for all students, so there was no way I was getting out of it even though I had managed to avoid it until my second year. I was beyond nervous. I did not know anyone in the class, and I was certain I would fail. Then I discovered something I never really noticed before. Maybe I was too wrapped up in my own panic before to pay attention. I finally noticed that nearly everyone else was nervous, too! Huh! I was no longer alone!!

We had to give three different types of speeches in that class. I managed to do all three fairly well. In fact, well enough to make an A. It was my first victory. I still was not very good, but I had learned how to talk from key bullet points and actually look at the audience. VICTORY! I lacked the natural flow of a great speaker, but I was happy with my progress. Although not so happy that I looked forward to speaking in public, yet satisfied I could actually make a presentation if necessary.

Couples training in speaking

Eventually my husband and I both started our careers, and he went on to present papers at conferences. To be totally honest, I would say that he also was not very good at speaking before groups. He would read word for word off an index card or try to memorize his speech. But who was I to judge! We took a speaking class together through one of those adult continuing education programs. Talk about your hot date night! We were both determined to become better speakers. I still am not sure why I wanted this, but I had that deep down feeling it was important and that it would somehow fit into my future plans.

With practice and the support of one another, we did get a little better. My husband went on to present quite a bit. And I used my nursing degree to help me get a position in the healthcare education department at the hospital where I worked. For both of us, speaking became a regular part of our jobs. While I was able to speak more and more, I would still get nervous, rush through my presentation, and stumble over my words. However, over the years I actually gave a few pretty darn good talks from time to time. When I think back, all of those were about something I really cared about. Hmm, was this linked to those magic tricks I could do without panic? I never really put that all together. What I was good at was putting together PowerPoint presentations. I could make the PowerPoint do amazing things that always got the attention of the audience. However, I still felt like I was not fully connecting with my audiences. I watched some of the other educators and tried to emulate them, but fear was still my constant companion in public speaking situations. UGH! Seriously, when was I going to get past this!?

Nothing like a crisis to move you forward
Then at 45 years old, after years of doing healthcare education in some shape or form, I was downsized out of a job.

While a shock at first, it was actually a blessing because it helped me uncover my passion. It led me to become a health coach. Now you may be thinking, "How does that figure into speaking?" It is actually what motivated me to really get on track with my journey to the stage. I decided I did not want to work for someone else again, and I started my own company. That meant I needed to promote myself and meet new people, so I began to attend networking events. If you know anything about networking, you know it is critical to have a good one-minute infomercial and also to be able to explain what you do to other people you meet. At events, I studied the best, especially those that always had people flock to them at the end of the event. And I started to learn and to rehearse. The difference between this speaking and the speaking I did before was that I cared 100% about this. It was my passion! I just had to share it! It was the magic from my childhood. When I spoke about things I cared about, I could battle past the fear.

I also started making short videos about health-related topics and worked hard to think of them as conversations with my best friend. I was getting better and better because my passion for the topic came through so clearly. If I messed up, I learned to work it into what I was doing. I found the videos really helped me practice. I never felt nervous making videos because I could always redo them or edit as needed.

Fear is about to get knocked out!

I still had one big area left to master. I wanted to be able to give live classes. Talking one-on-one was great, but I could only help so many people that way. I wanted to share the secrets to getting healthy for a lifetime with large groups of people. I wanted to make a big change! Yet the thought of standing in front of a big group and talking for anything more than a few moments took me right back to those school days of panic and tears. But I could NOT let that stop me. That little space deep down inside had become much bigger and was calling to me. It was telling me: "It is your time. You are meant to do this! You MUST master this to have the success you want and deserve!"

So off I went to a three-day speaking boot camp. I bravely stood in front of the crowd and quietly said in my head, "Fear, I see you," and then I punched it right in the face. I smiled and channeled my power and strength into convincing the entire room to buy into my group's fictitious *broccolicous* monthly broccoli shipment plan. It was my defining moment. I spoke with clarity, conviction, and passion. I acknowledged the fear and sent it packing. Don't get me wrong, I still feel that fear, but now I let it know I see it and it knows my fist is heading straight for it.

If you are reading this book, it is because you have something you want to say or share. You have your own magic! Do NOT let fear or shyness hold you back. The world needs to hear your message. It needs to hear your words. Develop your skills and work to improve your abilities. Then when that moment comes and you step to the front of the room, stand tall, smile, and if fear comes knocking, just PUNCH it in the FACE!

Janis David

teaches women to empower themselves through belly dancing combined with Qigong. In July 2013, Janis released her first Beginning Belly Dance instructional DVD, *Ageless Belly Dancing*, currently being used in the United States, Ireland, Japan and Germany. *Dance With Qi* offers private, semi-private and group lessons for Belly Dance and Qigong, as well as speaking engagements about women's sensuality. Learn to dance effortlessly regardless of age, size or shape. Watch for her new book *Escapades of a Belly Dancer, The Empath* by the summer of 2015.

Contact Janis at:
(850) 251-2192
Janis@dancewithqi.com
www.janisdavid.com

From Stage Fright to Performance Perfection

Janis David

During the summer of my 11th year, I was faced with a performance challenge. I had been taking dancing lessons since the age of 3, and at the age of 11, I was prepared to take the stage with a group of a dozen other young girls. Well, not really prepared but scheduled to perform. Our song came on and we all ran out to the stage in formation. I was the smallest girl and at one end of the line of dancers.

As soon as I looked out at the audience, I forgot my dance and wanted to run away. I had a bad case of stage fright! As I tried to inch my way back to the curtain, my teacher pushed me back out into the line. I had no choice but to follow along and try to breathe at the same time. I was in tears. The experience was traumatic and I never performed again as a child.

It wasn't until I was an adult that I realized my burning desire to dance on stage. I'd been belly dancing for close to 30 years and had over 75 different teachers, learning all different styles from different countries to different music. I knew how to dance and with all my classical training, dancing through high school and college, I knew I was a good dancer. When I attended the Haflas (Middle Eastern parties for performing) and watched other belly dancers dance solo or in a group, while I appreciated their particular talents and beauty, I believed I was a better dancer. It broke my heart that I was so afraid to dance on stage or dance in public with an audience.

This burning desire to dance was enough for me to speak to one of my favorite belly dance teachers and mentors. She had finally come to the realization that I was not a determined performer, that I was actually quite shy. I asked her how to get myself up on the stage. The first suggestion was Valium. But I couldn't take that and still stand up straight, let alone dance. The second suggestion was liquid courage. Now, that I could handle! I learned that vodka and tequila did wonders to quell my hammering heartbeat.

In my late 40's, I met a woman who had surgery and wanted to learn to belly dance as part of her physical therapy. In exchange for private instruction, she agreed to "make" me perform by my 50th birthday. We made our costumes, I choreographed our dance, and we performed together in another town at one of the Haflas. It was an ecstatic experience. I finally felt successful in my dancing. I did it! I got on stage and I danced and I loved it! I suppose it was the personal challenge that made me get on stage. It was a moment of growth, a way to share my love of dance with the audience and my fellow dancers. Through this effort I became a better teacher and developed more original choreography.

Belly dancing is my favorite form of dance. I combine belly dance with Modern Dance, Jazz and Ballet moves, along with Qigong Energy Movement in my own form of dance that I call *Dance With Qi.* When I was 58, inviting women to my workshops, I would hear some women say, "I'm too old" or "I'm too fat" to belly dance. Not. I would tell them my age and they could see that I was overweight. Belly dancing is not about shaking and jiggling. It's not all about the belly, although it is our belly, or our core, that allows us to dance this way. Hearing these comments, wanting to share my love of dance, trying to reach more women and teach them to love their bodies as they are, all propelled me into the world of video.

I decided to produce a video for women, women of all ages, shapes and sizes. I designed my set, rented an historical high school gym, hired a photographer to videotape, had musicians create original music and wrote my script. We filmed over a period of three days. The echo in the gym was awful so once the video was complete, I learned how to edit the video in a recording studio where we added the music after the fact, then I read my script by doing a voiceover. There was one beautiful performance to a favorite song of mine that I paid sync right fees to use the song without getting sued. Once the video was done, I produced it myself and have been using the DVD as promotional material and selling it as well.

The more I promoted my DVD, *Ageless Belly Dancing*, the more I spoke to women about the sensuality of belly dancing. How strong the connection is that I feel between belly dancing and Qigong energy work, how sensuous and alive I feel when I'm dancing and how that feeling carries on through my daily life. I am alive. I am sensuous. I am happy. It is these very wonderful feelings and ways to flow through life that I am determined to teach other women. I am writing my book *Escapades of a Belly Dancer, The Empath* as one way to describe the sensuality I feel. I speak to women about how to feel what I feel, how to breathe, how to develop and release internal muscles to reach the highest level of pleasure in our own bodies. It is my goal to teach women to empower themselves through *Dance With Qi* to regain and maintain their sensuality and sexuality. I want all women to be as happy, content and satisfied as I am in my sexuality and expression, and guide them to living a sensual life.

In essence, in my journey to the stage, I have arrived. I have conquered my stage fright with consistent practice and confidence (and a little bit of liquid courage). I have the clarity I need to be on stage and talk about women's bodies and know I will help many women learn to enjoy their own bodies, and to *Dance With Qi*, your pathway to pleasure.

"The best way for people to feel good about you is to help them feel good about themselves." ~ Trish Carr

Georgianna Rivera

is a Certified Professional Speaker and the Founder of Relationship Rx. She is passionately committed to helping successful women understand and transform their relationships. Her clients praise her for her work, which assists them to find a sense of empowerment, to trust in their ability to develop positive solutions and to find a path to peace and stability. Georgianna is certified as a Master Teacher in three well-known registered energy healing modalities (Reiki, Integrated Energy Therapy, and Magnified Healing), a celebrated Intuitive, and a Certified Akashic Records Professional Consultant. She brings the blending of this experience, knowledge and wisdom together in providing individual and unique solutions.

You can contact Georgianna at:
www.GeorgiannaRivera.com

Whom Do You Serve? Identifying Your Purpose for Speaking From the Stage

Georgianna Rivera

Who wants to be first?" A hand shot up immediately from across the room. "She's brave," I said to myself. "Or is it better to get it over and be done?" We were at speakers training, and we all wanted to be there.

As we each took our turn, stood up and faced our audience and spoke, the experience was universal. "How did that feel?" our skilled and talented instructor asked each one.

"I was a little nervous." Or maybe a lot, as evidenced by a red face, shaking hands, a trembling voice, and a surge of adrenaline that we were not quite experienced at handling.

This was normal. I remembered the well-known research study, as it was mentioned again from the front of the room. Public speaking is the number one fear cited by those polled on the topic. It was at the top of an impressive list of grotesque and blood-curdling experiences. Death was close to the bottom. Which means that seven out of ten people would rather die than stand on a stage and speak in public. Really? Is this a real fear or just a perception? Or should I say a misperception?

I found out. I took my turn at speaking. In my mind, I saw myself as confident and skilled, speaking with ease and nailing my presentation. Alas, it was universal. I was like everyone else. I felt the fear, the nervousness in the pit of my stomach and the urge to run away. But I spoke.

I heard examples of some very famous individuals who speak to thousands and yet they have their own system for relieving the anxiety. At least, I was in very good company. It was comforting to hear that public speaking is a skill that can be learned with knowledge and technique. Experience would bring confidence and wisdom in presenting myself to others. But I had to be willing to learn from the experience knowing that there would be bumps and bruises along the way.

I was compelled to ask myself these questions: *Why would I want to do this? What would make me place myself in this position?* I imagine all public speakers have had to ask themselves those same questions. If you are reading this book and thinking of becoming a speaker, you will ask yourself and listen to the answers.

This is how I answered: *Purpose, Passion, Mission, and Love.* That love included love for others, and also love for myself.

Purpose

I am here for a purpose. That purpose has been in many different places over my lifetime. At one point, it meant being the best nurse I could be and serving my patients with love, integrity and skill; and I had a most marvelous career. In my new life, it is supporting others through my business, helping them to heal through the power of meditation and transforming their thoughts, and also assisting others to look at the core of their relationship difficulties with honesty and set a healing course with new goals for their lives. I found this purpose because I lived this purpose. I have experienced everything I teach to others, which I know prepared me to serve this unique role. In order to serve, I have to find those I can help and they have to find me. Speaking from the stage is ideal for this reason.

I believe everyone is here for a purpose. Our skills, talents and life experiences have prepared us to find our place.

So, I ask, "What is your purpose?"

Passion

Passion is a feeling, and a most incredible emotion to enjoy. It feels like flying, soaring above the rooftops as the wind supports you and gently brings you back to earth again. It is the fuel that keeps you going when you thought your energy was gone. It helps you to work those long hours in order to move your business forward. You believe in yourself and what you do because of your passion. That feeling is proof of being in alignment with who you truly are and it will serve you in times of difficulty until you are successful in that which you wish to achieve.

You can always spot a speaker who is passionate about his or her message. It's that intangible quality we all can recognize in others. How important is it to nourish and fan the flames of our own passion for our purpose?

In that sense, allowing our passion to show through as we speak is desired. Can passion relieve the fear and anxiety of speaking from the stage? If our mind and thoughts are on our passion, there won't be room for anything negative.

Are you enjoying your passion?

Mission

Mission speaks of what you, and only you, are individually here to accomplish. Just like no two snowflakes are alike, no two humans are alike. The combination of DNA with all its variations and your life experiences has formed you into a one-of-a-kind person. There will never be another you on this earth again. That has always amazed me that there will never be another me again.

You are a gift, and a gift that only you can give. You can reach certain people in a way that no one else ever could, just as there are those who touch our hearts and help us to heal our lives like no other. This holds true no matter what we choose to do with our lives, be it in a small circle of influence or a much greater circle when we choose to speak from the stage. Speaking from the stage puts us front and center in life. We are showing up and an important part of success is just showing up.

How are you showing up in life?

Love

Certainly, we all recognize that love for others and wanting to serve are driving forces in our actions and in our businesses. But can we also look at love for self as a motivating factor? Actually our love for others stems from our own self-love.

Life is meant to be lived in an expansive way. We are evolving, moving forward to higher and higher states of consciousness. Life begets life. When we reach for that expansiveness by moving ourselves forward, we align with the principles of the Universe. When we shrink back in fear or allow the risks to stop us in our tracks, we lessen or contract our life force energy and the Universe responds to our actions.

There is a line from an affirmation I say daily. And it goes like this: "The river of life never stops flowing, and it flows through me with lavish expression."

Would you like to be in a position of having this rich life force flowing to you bringing the abundance you deserve? I would. This is showing love for myself by growing and reaching for more. For me this means saying *Yes* to the opportunity to speak from the stage.

And so, I ask, "Are you showing love for yourself by reaching for more in your life?"

Allison Ronis

has been tinkering with computers since she was 15 years old. In the summer of 1998, Allison found two broken computers and decided that she could make one working computer out of two broken ones. She was successful, and ever since then she has followed her passion. Through self-education and formal schooling, she learned everything she knows today to share with the world. A former teacher and trainer, Allison has taken her skills to the next level. She completed her Master of Science Degree in 2015. She is a Graphic Artist and Tech Specialist whose passion is to help others find their inner techie (she believes everyone has that in them).

You can contact Allison at:
(954) 839-0563
allisonronis@gmail.com
http://girlsguide2technology.com

A Bull in a China Shop

Allison Ronis

Growing up I was always the center of attention and most of the time it was because I was into something I shouldn't have been. One could say I was courageous, brave, outgoing and forthcoming, but in the late '60's they just called it hyperactive and reckless. If something crashed, my mother or father or any family member who was around including cousins, would come running from anywhere in the house bellowing my name, wondering what I had gotten myself into this time. Things crashed and Allison was to blame. Often, I heard my family talking about what Allison had gotten into recently, and I was nicknamed a bull in a china shop.

Growing up like that never inhibited me. I always looked life in the eye and jumped forward, never thinking. I said what I said, I did what I did and didn't care what impact it had on me or anyone or anything. I went forth, full steam ahead throughout life, never caring or giving my actions a second thought, unless my actions or my words were pointed out to me, and more often than not, my actions and my words were pointed out to me as aggressive or mean. I was told I lacked a filter. Bosses, friends, family would tell me, "Allison, you've got to slow down," "Allison, you're aggressive and abrasive," "Allison, be careful," "Allison, you move too fast" or "Allison, you have no filter." I never listened. I rolled my eyes and thought they were crazy and that I was fine and if they didn't like me or my words or my actions, then, oh, well. The reality was things were not fine. I either quit or got fired from every job I ever had, and no job ever lasted more than a year. Plus my relationships across the board were covered in ick. I fought with people, argued with people, yelled, threw temper tantrums, you name it. I did it to get my way. It is not pretty to see a grown woman throwing a temper tantrum.

I never thought I was going to go to college. I barely made it through high school, and after graduation, I went straight to work. For several years, I was a teacher in a day care center. Then one day I woke up and thought, "I don't want to spend my entire life making minimum wage." I wanted more and I was ready and open. I was living on my own and, for the first time in my life, I knew things had to start changing. Shortly after my 21st birthday, I asked my mom if I could move back home with her to start junior college. She let me, and one small shift started to occur. I was taking my life into my own hands for the first time.

In junior college, I began to emerge. I took leadership classes and found my love for theatre. I was finally being accepted for who I was. One summer I applied to take a summer class at New York University. To my surprise, I was accepted and off I went to New York City by myself. I spent seven weeks there, enjoying my life and my education. After that experience, I came home and decided to see about furthering my education in New York City. I applied to Pace University and was accepted into their bachelor's program and again off I went on my own. My mother still believes this was the bravest thing I've ever done.

Throughout my time at Pace, I was in a couple of shows. I have always admired actors. What I loved most about actors is they always had the right thing to say at the right time, and what they said moved people to laughter or to tears. I knew I moved people, but it was mostly to frustration, anger or tears. I wanted to change that more than anything else. I wanted to make people happy, to be someone of influence, but I had no idea how. I still believed I was a bull in a china shop, abrasive and aggressive, and no matter what happened I was still told the same thing: "Allison, you've got to slow down," "Allison, you're aggressive and abrasive," "Allison, be careful," "Allison, you move too fast," or "Allison, you have no filter." It was infuriating to me. I knew that it was all true. Yet I was still that bull in a china shop not knowing how to change, so onward I went. This was who I was and I had to accept it, knowing all the while I needed to change in order for things to change.

I remember one of my professors encouraging me to audition for the lead in an upcoming play. I honestly believed at the time that he was pulling my leg so I never tried out for the part. I was afraid of making a fool of myself. I still believed I was a bull in a china shop, and that I was aggressive and abrasive. And I still wasn't changing. I had many conflicts with others during that time, which kept those beliefs in place. At the same time, I also believed I was a leader. Talk about being conflicted! I stayed behind the scenes and became a stage manager. I loved doing that; however, after a few years of stage managing, I again felt unhappy, so I left that profession.

I started working in the technology industry. I had always loved computers. My first and only A in high school was in a computer class. This had been a secret passion of mine for many years. As a hobby, I learned to repair computers. A boss at a well-known publishing company took me under her wing and gave me a chance. During that time, I started to look at other people and how they behaved. I started to shift my thinking and my behaviors. For the next few years, I began to learn everything I could about technology, soaking up information and watching others. I learned a lot about people and technology during that time but began to miss home.

In the winter of 2003, I moved back home to Florida. I began teaching Drama in the public school system. I was very good at it. It took three years for me to become "burned out." I say that because the real reason I quit was that I wanted more, plus all of my relationships at school were packed with conflict because of my behaviors and attitude.

I joined a financial services company that promised me riches and freedom, something I had wanted for many years. I hated having a boss. I hated people telling me what to do or how to act or when to show up. I wanted freedom and this company sold me on having that, so I quit teaching. I saw this as a way out, and I took this business on as any bull in a china shop would, full speed ahead, full time. I made no money, but for the first time I had freedom.

This decision to quit teaching and become a full-time entrepreneur cost me a personal relationship, one I was very fond of. It hurt a lot. For the very first time, I realized that my actions and my behaviors really did affect me and the people around me. I had always known this, but it had never affected me as much as it did this time. So much so that, for the first time, I made a conscious effort to change. I started to listen to the suggestions of others as to how to behave, how to dress, and how to speak. Most of all, I learned to shut up and listen. So I listened and learned and obeyed.

At the same time two of the most influential women in my life, my aunts, Trish Carr and Nancy Matthews, were up to something big. They were creating a wonderful company (Women's Prosperity Network) bringing women together. Nancy and Trish have always been strong positive presences in my life, along with other aunts and uncles, parents, cousins, and friends who loved me no matter what and wanted the best for me. I managed to have many people love me unconditionally no matter what I broke or what I said along the way. These women and men always encouraged me to be positive and look beyond my circumstances.

I started to see people around me excelling. I saw Nancy and Trish doing extraordinary things, and I wanted to play with them. I wanted to be them. One day I was ready. My father always said, "When the student is ready the teacher will appear." So I realized that, for things to change, I had to change. I quit the financial services industry. It was never a passion of mine, yet helping and serving others was. Technology was a passion, and I was good at it. I started showing up at events, surrounding myself with men and women who were up to big things. I started to invest in myself and in my business. I knew that if I wanted to play with the big girls, I needed to play full out and give it my all. My mind had to shift from employee mentality to entrepreneur mentality, and when I started to think differently and listen more, my business took off. It wasn't enough for me to sit back and watch people that I admired playing big. I wanted to play, too.

It has taken many years for me to find my power and overcome that "bull in a china shop" mentality. And as I keep moving forward in my power and strength, listening to others, I shift from a girl who was aggressive and abrasive and lacked

Allison Ronis

a filter to a woman who listens more, filters her words, serves others, and is kind to anyone and everyone. The bull in the china shop disappears and what shows up is a strong powerful successful woman.

"You have the ultimate power to control the quality of your life, your relationships and your destiny. You have this power in each moment ... it is the power of choice."
~ Nancy Matthews

Catherine 'Cat' Wagman

is President of Working Words, Inc. (FL). She always makes it a point to put her clients at ease, treats them with respect, and looks forward to sharing moments of laughter and appreciation for their vision, work experiences, and expertise. Her perceptive talents boost each client's awareness, so they can more easily identify what they want to accomplish and create plans of action. She is also an entertaining speaker, a creative writing workshop facilitator, and the author of *"Why ... THANK YOU! — How to Have Fun Writing Fantastic Notes and More."*

For additional information, please contact Cat at:
(954) 629-8772
Cat@CatWagman.com
www.CatWagman.com

The Message Propels the Messenger

Cat Wagman

When I was a kid I dreaded getting up in front of the class. Three incidents in particular happened in fifth grade. The first was when I was to introduce a friend's mother and for the life of me I couldn't wrap my tongue around her name, Mrs. Dougherty. No matter how many times I practiced writing and saying it, when the time came, what I said definitely started with a "D" and ended with a "y" and everything else in between was a mess.

The second was when it was my turn to read the answers aloud from the back of the math book, so my classmates could check their work. One boy took extreme pleasure in correcting how I said one answer, to whatever thousandth decimal point it was.

The third was during a class spelling bee and the word I was given was "any." Simple, right? As I thought about its spelling and saw it clearly in my mind, I confidently said the first letter ... "N!" The cruel laughter that erupted compounded the ridicule and my humiliation of being the first one who had to sit down.

Over the years, with similar incidents like these, my desire to step into the spotlight was further tempered with fear and doubt.

My secret dreams of becoming an actress were quashed due to my propensity for not being able to memorize even the simplest of lines (a first grade class play memory) without my stress-triggered dyslexia scrambling my words.

Puppets to the Rescue!

In sixth grade I had a much different experience when it came time to perform my part in the class play, a puppet production of *"Peter and the Wolf."* My teacher agreed to my request to play the part of the cat; and as I put the puppet on my hand, it was as if I had a whole new brain, one which actually coordinated the memorizing with the spoken words. Though my name was listed in the program, no one could actually *see* me, because I was hidden behind the puppet theater stage. As with this puppet and the many others I've purchased, I found each one to be a natural extension of my personality and its eclectic collection of alter egos.

This made me realize, instead of aspiring to be *in* the spotlight, perhaps I would work better behind the scenes. It was also around this time that I found other ways to express my creativity through art and writing.

Now, please understand, I never was a wallflower by any means. My comedic side is quick to pick up on any cue. What I loved was having people laugh *with* me, not at me. And when I embraced my innate talent — the gift of laughter — it started to turn my attitude around about being in the spotlight ... maybe ... just a little.

Then the Ocean Called My Name ...

I'm sure that I'm not the only girl from the mid-1960's who fell in love with Luke Halpin and Flipper, the bottle-nosed dolphin. During each summer vacation on Long Beach Island on the New Jersey shore, I loved watching pods of dolphins swim just beyond the breakers. That's when I decided I wanted to become a marine biologist and study sharks and dolphins.

I entered University of Miami (FL) with high expectations, until I discovered the formaldehyde permeating the biology lab was one of my migraine triggers. Suddenly, I was left with wondering, *"Now, what am I going to do?"*

I had always been interested in electronics, because I helped my Dad build his Heathkit® projects. So I joined the university's Concert Sound Crew. I was the only girl *WORKING*, laying the cables and wires around the stage. Many of the guys also worked as DJs at the campus radio station, WVUM, 90.5 FM. The following year when I became the station's Director of Continuity, I switched my major to Communications.

Behind the Scenes in Public Television

After graduation, I worked at WPBT/Channel 2, the South Florida PBS station. As one of the *original* Muppets fans, I loved going to work each morning and turning onto Sesame Street (aka NE 20th Avenue) in North Miami Beach. Since I worked in the Program Operations Department, we were required to have a television on so we could monitor what was being broadcast. Throughout the day I could hear the kid programs playing in the background, each with their own set of memorable characters, including the Muppets!

One day, someone asked why I didn't work in FRONT of the camera, since I was pretty and had a great speaking voice. I immediately answered, "I'm more comfortable working behind the scenes." Still, it got me thinking about the spotlight again.

Cutting My Speaker's Eye Teeth in the Classroom

So much can change in a few short years, especially when I knew I wanted to be a stay-at-home Mom. Prior to the births of my sons and, because I didn't want to get calls while I was knee-deep in diapers, I wrote detailed procedures manuals documenting my jobs at WPBT and at Fred Hunter Funeral Homes. I also used them to train my future replacements. After the birth of my second son, Bernie, I shifted gears again, taking on freelance writing projects, and in 1989, I established Working Words, Inc.

When my elder son, Devin, started at Pembroke Pines Elementary, I decided to become a volunteer SPEAKER for their annual Career Days. He and his brother were five years apart academically, because of their birthdays, so my tenure covered about ten years.

I've always been passionate about writing and wanted to inspire the kids to trust their imaginations and test their writing talents. With each presentation, I used whatever freelance writing project I had recently completed. And as the years went by my list of speaking topics grew from *"What is a Freelance Writer?", "What If? and How Come? — 2 Great Story Writing Techniques,"* and *"How Scriptwriting Tells The Camera Where to Look"* to *"Time and Project Management Tips"* and *"Writing for Your Future."*

In the interim, I was invited to a Florida Freelance Writers Association Annual Conference where I spoke about *"How to Establish Your Identity as a Writer"* and *"How to Write a Simple Procedure Manual."*

From Class Volunteer to Published Author

In 1990, I did my first *Why ... THANK YOU!* FUNshop for Devin's third grade class. It was so successful; it became my go-to presentation as I traveled around to area schools where I shared the following three basic ideas with the kids and teachers:

To think of a thank-you note as a mini-adventure in creative writing,

All Mom is looking for is three to five sentences, and

It's perfectly okay to use your imagination and sense of humor.

Later, in 1997, I published "*Why ... THANK YOU!* — How to Have Fun Writing Fantastic Notes and More," the only guide for kids and grown-ups that uses thank-you notes to teach creative writing. With the publicity I was able to generate, more opportunities to speak came my way — from newspaper, magazine, and radio interviews to appearances at Levenger®, Barnes & Noble®, Borders®, and various book shows. Professional organizations started asking me, too. Soon, my *"Leap into Creative Writing"* and *"Creative Passion in Action"* workshops began sparking the interests of beginning and experienced writers.

Conquering the Chaos

While I have a highly functional Right Brain/Creative side, I also have an equally pragmatic Left Brain/Processes and Procedures aspect. And as I move into doing more speaking again, I have discovered a great need for the simple technique I developed and perfected to document office procedures.

Many entrepreneurs and small business owners work hard to build their businesses all by themselves. Then, they reach a point where they can't do *everything* any more, nor do they want to. The added stress, resentment, and how crazy it gets when they are absent just makes it worse.

I show them how to write down those how-to's currently locked inside their brains, and then once their operational procedures are in place, they discover it's easier to delegate, training others becomes faster, and they can quickly determine which jobs to outsource.

Imagine being able to reclaim your valuable time and devote your creative energies doing the things you really love to do for your clients, too.

Beyond Today

Now, I aspire to be an Entertaining Educator who Enlightens my audiences. Sure, I may have an occasional dyslexic moment, which I'll be able to handle better with grace, ease, and perhaps a laugh or two.

Still, it all comes back to the message that sits deep in your soul, the one that will move you to speak. My message, the one I truly believe in is ...

*"When it starts at the top, **A**ppreciation, **R**espect, and **T**rust will transform any business." ~ Cat Wagman*

"Remember when life was all fun and games? It still is! It's all in your perception. Choose it and be happy."
~ Trish Carr

Jenny Battig

is passionate about helping people renew their healthy mind and body balance naturally. She is a Certified Clinical Hypnotherapist with the International Association of Interpersonal Hypnotherapists.

Prior to pursuing hypnotherapy in 2013, Jenny worked as a Human Factors Engineer for over 15 years. Even as a Human Factors Engineer, her goal was to understand what people really needed so she could help maximize their productivity. Now she helps people understand and reach their maximum potential by tapping into their subconscious to efficiently uncover and transform the beliefs and emotions that have held them back.

Find out more at www.epicrenewal.com.

My Journey to the Stage

Jenny Battig

Having been raised in a conservative, relatively small town in southwest Ohio, I would have never guessed that I'd be on my way to speaking to hundreds, even thousands, of people in Florida and around the country, sharing something as significant as the power that we all have to heal ourselves. The universe has mysterious ways of bringing us to our calling. This feels like the perfect time for me to step into my passion to help others understand how much power they truly have over their own health and happiness!

It wasn't that I didn't think I was smart enough or that the thought of public speaking freaked me out. I am a Leo, a natural born leader, and I am an oldest child, so it's not uncommon for us to get more used to stepping out and doing something on our own. I got good grades in school, had some natural athletic ability and could carry a tune, so I'll admit I didn't have to struggle as much as some did to make it through those years. However, the idea of dreaming big was not something that came naturally to me. The only big dream I remember having as a kid was to play volleyball in the Olympics. Why? Because I loved to play volleyball and wanted to play from a young age. I'm not sure if I tended to dream small due to being raised Catholic (and the way I internalized the guilt complex), or the fact that my family had to go through many years of penny pinching to make ends meet, or even the conservative nature of where I was raised... not a lot (meaning none that I know of) of millionaires in my hometown and we rarely travelled out of town except for the occasional trip to "the mall" in Dayton or to see a Reds baseball game in Cincinnati.

As I got older, I realized the Olympics wasn't going to happen for me because it took a LOT more work and focus than what I would be able to follow through with, but I did at least get to play volleyball at a small NCAA Division I school in Dayton, Ohio. College started to shift my thinking some. I started out wanting to major in Accounting because I'd been told I was meticulous and I knew I was good at math. It didn't take long before I realized Accounting wasn't for me. Thanks to one of my volleyball teammates I learned about Human Factors Engineering. The more I found out about it, the more it appealed to me, so I followed my intuition and switched majors (several people thought I was a little crazy for switching *from* Business *to* Engineering, but I knew it was the right direction for me). In case you haven't heard of Human Factors Engineering, it involves understanding and taking into consideration the capabilities and limitations of humans when designing or developing the products or systems they will be interacting with. The main things that I liked about it was it meant learning about what humans were capable of, then designing things to be more efficient and safe for them to use.

The other shift that I noticed in college was that, in getting out of my small town and going to a bigger city and a bigger school, surrounded by a lot of new people, I felt a bit out of my league. Getting good grades and being a student athlete weren't as significant in this case, so I realized I was somewhat reserved or shy around most people. I felt more comfortable in small groups and even that was better after I felt I really knew the people in the group. The years of growing up with all the same kids in your classes and on your sports teams were over. Welcome to the real world, Jenny!

So, starting my career as an engineer felt comfortable because it seemed to be working mostly alone or in small groups and it paid good money. In my case I ended up being involved primarily with user interface design and got hired by a company in Melbourne, Florida. The only reason I even considered a move like that was because Human Factors Engineering was a fairly unique niche and most of the jobs in the Dayton area had already been taken by those who graduated before me. Plus my college boyfriend had moved to Florida and I'd been to visit him a couple times and it seemed like a pretty nice place to live (especially compared to Ohio). Making that leap, to move nearly a thousand miles away from where I'd lived my whole life to live by myself and start a new career was a tough one, but just like I'm glad I changed from Accounting to Human Factors Engineering for my degree, I'm definitely glad I made the decision to move to Florida, too.

Throughout my 15+ years as an engineer, I not only got to design efficient user interfaces, I got to train users on how to use the software applications and was able to communicate with the end users as well as the software engineers, often becoming a translator to help bridge the gap in knowledge between those groups. So I got some experience presenting to small groups in those jobs, but nothing I was really passionate about.

As I entered my late 30's I was doing pretty well career-wise, but had been struggling with weight gain for at least a decade (not uncommon for college athletes as they transition to desk jobs). That struggle kept me on the sidelines or in the background most of the time. I didn't date or go out much, let alone look for opportunities to get in front of crowds to speak.

I finally decided to try something radical after a hypnotherapist did a "lunch 'n learn" presentation at my company. I loved the analogy she used about the mind being similar to a computer. The conscious mind is like the applications we use (for documents, spreadsheets, graphics programs, etc.) and the subconscious is like all the programming that goes on underneath that that makes it work. So, like you can't just type into a document or spreadsheet 'go faster' and expect your computer's performance to improve on its own, in the conscious mind, a similar command is unlikely to fix unwanted behaviors or long-term habits. Instead, you need to get to the programming layer and possibly remove some corrupted files so it can get back to optimal performance, which translates to needing to access the subconscious mind to reprogram and resolve any old corrupted memories or beliefs that have been holding us back without us even knowing it. Makes sense, right?

As a result of those hypnotherapy sessions I lost over 80 pounds in the course of a couple years and was inspired to break out of the world of what was feeling like corporate slavery at that point to pursue my passion and share with others how to tap into their true potential.

I'd also read a few books that further substantiated how powerful our minds are when we give them the proper support and clear out the garbage. That helped solidify my plans for my next big jump in life. When I became a Certified Clinical Hypnotherapist, I started off trying some typical advertising techniques to get clients I could help on an individual basis. While I had some amazing successes with clients, I felt like what I was doing was a well-kept secret (and it shouldn't be a secret). As I became aware of additional resources for entrepreneurs, I joined some networking groups and started to take more workshops and get more coaching from people who were very successful. It became clear to me that in order to help a LOT more people renew their healthy mind/body balance, I needed to sharpen my speaking skills. For me it's not just about being able to help people finish their journey to greater health and happiness, it's about waking them up to the possibilities so they can start that journey, whether it be with me or some other holistic health practitioner.

I had been doing some classes on essential oils for small audiences and had a multi-day course in some amazing techniques to improve social emotional intelligence, but neither of those seemed to be catching on and getting people's attention.

Learning the tools to be an effective speaker has been a true boost of confidence and inspiration for me as I get ready to jump into the next chapter of my career doing workshops and retreats. I'm so grateful that I'm being led down this amazing path to impact more lives in a more powerful and positive way than I ever could have dreamed as a kid!

Beverly Sorrells

is a licensed acupuncture physician practicing in South Florida. She is also a member of the Foundation for Wellness Professionals, a nonprofit organization of healthcare professionals who donate their time in their respective communities speaking on health and wellness. On the water, Beverly is a competitive and endurance paddler, continually practicing her sport in dragon boats and outrigger canoes.

A freelance writer on the side, she is also working on her newest blog, www.theNakedProject.net.

Bouncing Back: How I Learned to Own My Space

Beverly Sorrells

The Program Director went down the checklist at the start of our class. "Halfway through the program you will be assigned a topic to research and, in the final module, you will give a 20-minute presentation to your classmates on your findings." I immediately felt a sense of panic rising in my throat. How could this be? Why can't we just turn in a written report like we will for all the other modules?

I quickly tuned her out as I tried to plot my next steps. I had recently started an accelerated degree completion program at a small, local college with the intent of escaping the medical billing world once I received my bachelor's degree. Now the thought of getting up in front of 20-plus people and speaking made me want to vomit. I had managed to get along perfectly well through school and work without having to give speeches and was quite happy hanging in the background and doing my thing. Besides, it was hard for me to even raise a question or make a comment during class. I totally sucked at thinking fast on my feet and others usually beat me to whatever it was I was going to say.

And now this. *Dear God, WHY???*

As I sat there contemplating the pros and cons of dropping out of the program (oh, yes I did!), I realized I had a decision to make: either I could let this thing defeat me now or I could take on this challenge and hope and pray that in 12 months I would be comfortable enough to get through the presentation without making a complete idiot of myself.

I chose the latter.

It's Always Something

Let's face it - we've all had our demons growing up; mine just happened to hang out there on public display.

When I was in elementary school, we didn't have honors or Advanced Placement classes. Instead, kids were "double-promoted." I was one of those kids, leapfrogging over second grade after I had switched schools and found myself royally bored to tears in the classroom.

While that move provided me with a good challenge on an academic level, it made life difficult socially. I was, in some cases, up to one and one-half years younger than my classmates. Believe me when I say that amount of time is HUGE for any third or fourth grader to navigate.

The end result? I was bullied in school. Mercilessly. So much so that one of my teachers had to stop her lesson and defend me during class one day. Of course, the full impact of bullying was lost amongst the faculty in that day, let alone knowing what the hell to do about it. Thus I would go to school, endure the taunts, and then go home and cry.

Fortunately I had a mother who was brave enough to take me to a psychologist, willing to wear what was then considered a badge of shame. From those visits I learned to set boundaries and began to express my mind.

Through all this I also learned to maintain a low profile, which became my modus operandi for several years. Not one to run with the popular crowd, I was quite happy within my own little tribe, contented to be a team member rather than a team leader and one of many voices in the choir yet never one of the soloists. And on and on and on.

Unfortunately I carried this mentality over to the working world. The scars from the careless judgment of my peers - that of my supposedly not being good enough - took years to completely heal. However, the resulting scar tissue remains. Even now, the larger the crowd, the quieter I tend to become.

Time Changes All Things

At some point along the way I got tired of missing out on opportunities. I began to volunteer, to speak up and to participate. I taught the senior girls' class in the Youth Group at my church. I became a Girl Scout leader when my daughter's troop lost its leader to a move. I traveled internationally with a lot of people I barely knew.

Yet public speaking still did not sit well with me. I usually managed to dodge it but, in the few times I could not, I pretty much went down in flames. It was not a lovely sight.

Rather, it was like being in fourth grade all over again.

A funny thing happens though, when you decide to challenge yourself: the more you attempt something, the easier it becomes. You discover an inner reserve that you didn't even know you had. And, if you're lucky, you might even begin to enjoy it.

That college presentation I dreaded? I ended up speaking on the oh-so-sexy topic of mankind's predestination versus free will. I wish I could say that I rehearsed extensively, but I didn't. I got up there, took in a deep breath, smiled and started out with a funny question about what I was wearing. That was enough to break the ice and get them laughing, which, in turn, relaxed all of us. Suddenly I was among friends.

That 20 minutes disappeared in a heartbeat as I was flipping overheads and giving my personal thoughts on five-point Calvinism. At the end, I earned positive feedback from my classmates as well as an A for my efforts. And for the first time I felt like I had left the last of my childhood baggage at the door and actually "owned" my space.

Lessons Learned

Fast forward to four years ago, when I left the corporate world to go back to school: little did I realize that I was getting into a profession that would require putting myself out there in public on a regular basis.

Although Chinese medicine is becoming more mainstream, there is still a lot of misconception regarding just how it works. Quite a few patients are wary of the acupuncture needles and some are distrusting of Chinese herbs. I find myself continually educating people about Chinese medical theory and the variety of problems acupuncture can heal. I also give talks on holistic ways to stay healthy via whole food nutrition, exercise and the use of essential oils.

Over the years I've learned a lot regarding public speaking. Specifically, I've learned that you have to:

Get out there and talk anywhere. To anyone. At anytime. Remember what I said about how the more you do something, the easier it becomes? Practice speaking at businesses as well as community and networking groups. Practice makes perfect - especially when it comes to public speaking!

Talk about what you love. When you are passionate about or really believe in something, it shows. And when you come from the point of sharing what you've learned, it automatically takes the emphasis off you and puts it where it belongs: with the audience.

Hone your craft. Take the time to read up on ways to better convey your message. Watch speakers for tips on what to do (and what not to do). Take workshops or join a local speakers group such as Toastmasters International.

Recently I gave a presentation to my largest audience yet. As one of the breakout speakers, I addressed a group of nearly 40 contractors at their annual convention. Who would've thought, right? I was prepared, stayed within my allotted time limit and taught them three secrets to a healthy life.

Was I nervous going in? Absolutely. Did I receive a question I wasn't prepared for? You bet. But in the end it turned out well.

I shared what I knew from my heart center.

People listened, asked questions and learned.

And yes, I actually enjoyed it.

Licia Berry

is an educator with a 25+ year career spanning public schools, state departments, and non-profit, corporate, and private sectors. In private practice since 2001, she supports others in awakening to their unique purpose, vision and mission. Informed by studies in energy dynamics, psychology, systems theory, family dynamics, quantum mechanics, neuroscience, creative arts, culture, and shamanism, Licia works in Whole Brain Synthesis to expand the use of our brains in co-creating the world we want. In 2013, she had the "divine opportunity" to put her knowledge to the test in supporting the complete recovery of her oldest son from a traumatic brain injury that almost took his life. Licia offers opportunities for discovery, insight, and leadership through group offerings, e-learning, and private consulting internationally. Licia resides in Tallahassee, Florida, where she runs her global online teaching practice and offers workshops and retreats.

Learn more at:
http://liciaberry.com
http://berrytrip.us

The Voice Is an Answer

Licia Berry

It's my mission that all people on the planet feel that they belong here, that it is no accident that they are born the way they are.

My advocacy has spanned many causes, from children to people with disabilities, to LGBTQ, to people of color, to survivors of violence and sexual assault, to women all over the globe.

I grew up in the south, a sensitive, observant girl in a culture that would perfectly prepare me to write and publish volumes of work about the human condition. In my childhood I experienced abuse of many kinds and lived in an environment of turmoil. This was a challenge to my spirit, a kind of *alchemical container* in which I was purified and evolved.

Having lived through my challenges, it is now my duty to speak about them. I believe it is not a coincidence that I have a passion for equality, respect and dignity for all people, and that I feel compelled to speak about it whenever possible.

But as an adult and woman who is determined to use her voice in the world, I must work constantly to keep my throat open. I am polite and kind, as a southern woman is raised to be. I'm also very sensitive to fear about speaking out because I was enculturated to be silent. I have an internal conflict when

I feel called to express my voice in a group setting. The temptation to shut it down is innate, strong, as if my life depends on it. My voice was perhaps the first casualty of my upbringing.

I had an internal experience some years ago as I was writing *SOUL COMPOST – Transforming Adversity into Spiritual Growth*; it was a kind of visualization, in which I saw that my voice went into a "cage" as a means of survival. In my inner vision, I saw my voice as a bird:

The bird in my throat wants to fly. It beats against the cage with its wings. My fear wants to tell the great bird to go to sleep. Goodness, it is a big bird. A giant bird. How on earth did it fit in that little cage? It must be so uncomfortable, so tight. It is here that I see that the great bird in my throat is an Eagle. The ferocity with which it meets my eyes is unmistakable. It WILL be heard. I fumble with the latch of the cage, and the great Eagle rushes the door as fast as I can open it. It pushes past me and alights, towering, by my side. It begins to screech like it has been silent for 5000 years; it screeches and calls and screams as if to break open the world with the sound. I am completely in awe of its voice and its powerful determination to speak. I make a vow to never ask this immense, warrior-like creature to step into the cage again. In fact, inspired by its ferocity, I pick up a giant sledgehammer and destroy the cage, watching as the pieces fly and scatter to the four winds. The Great Eagle observes my actions, approving with its proud eyes. This bird is free.

This inner experience helped me to understand that there was no accident in my experience of challenging things and that I was "designed" to live through them in order to share my experience. My life has molded me to be a voice for equality just as surely as I feel compelled to talk about my vision of sharing power. It is no accident that I am the way I am or that I have passion for my mission - that all people on the planet know they are a unique and vital part of the architectural design of our evolution and humanity's existence. What I've learned is that *our voice is a direct answer to questions posed by life.* As I wrote in my 2012 book, *SOUL COMPOST*:

> "*The power of our voice is misunderstood. We think of the voice as a means to an end, the way to communicate what we want and to get it. But the voice is so much more profound than a mere tool for attainment of our desires.*
>
> "*It is the expression of our spirit. The voice is the vehicle through which sound vibration travels in the body to uniquely express our core essence. Have you noticed that some people's voice really makes you want to listen to them? Those voices are clear expressions of that person's unique purpose on the earth. Have you noticed that some words are more powerful coming from some people than others? Those words that ring so true are coming from that person's essence, their direct connection to their spirit. When someone is speaking and you can't pay attention or someone is constantly interrupted when they're speaking, it is because the power of spirit is not in their voice. I think of the throat as a direct door to the Voice of the Creator.*"

I was afraid to use my voice because I was trained to be silent. It was a survival mechanism that served me until I was strong enough to break the pattern and reach beyond my conditioning. Over the years I continued to find myself in situations where I had to take a stand, but I was so terrified that I couldn't share the truth and people could not understand my wisdom or receive my point of view. I worried about others' approval of my words, and painfully, I was frequently misunderstood or maligned. But I lived with this rather than to be exposed and naked to criticism or assault. Obviously, survival patterns from my childhood made me think I would die if I spoke my heart!

But now, I feel I'll die if I DON'T speak up and use my voice to address my concerns about the world. And I feel the encouragement of the people who are looking for my voice in the confusion and competing noise of our modern society. It is starting to dawn on me...the clearer I am in what I say, the greater the amplification of my message, and this is how I will help other people awaken to their *own* unique vision. *My free voice will call to other voices locked in cages.* The courage to use my voice can liberate others' voices.

If you are passionate about a cause, if you have something weighing on your heart, if you feel a push from the inside to speak or share what you see, then you are speaking God's voice (however you define it.) You were meant to be an instrument of change and to inspire.

A woman said to me recently after hearing me speak, "I didn't know the words to describe my feelings, but you just articulated them. You gave me words for something I haven't been able to express; your words are a gift to me and to women who haven't found their voice yet. You are a courageous woman; thank you for the light you shine in the world."

I support my clients and students in finding their unique voice and purpose. Again, I feel it is no accident that we are the way we are; our design is an answer to a question posed by life, a response to a problem seeking a solution. It is my greatest joy to watch someone wake up to their inherent perfection, to realize the congruence of their life experiences and the destiny they are meant to live, and to allow the greater wisdom of life to express through them in the world.

As I learned, the things that happen to us in this life are not because we are "bad" or "deserved" them...the things that happened to us in our lives are the very crucible in which we become what we must become. We are being called forward to answer life's asking.

Linda Allred

is the co-author of the best-selling book, *Answering the Call,* published by Celebrity Press. The book became an instant #1 Best-Seller on Amazon the day it was released and allows readers to Answer Their Own Call in their life journey, whether that's losing 10lbs-100lbs, reducing stress, quitting smoking or making $100,000-$1,000,000 in their business. Based on the success of the book, Linda was awarded a Quilly™ Award in September, 2014, in Hollywood, CA, where she also presented a powerful presentation in front of more than 200 Best-Selling Authors.

You can learn more about Linda at www.LindaAllred.com.

How I Became the Hottest Ticket in Town at 74!

Linda Allred

It still amazes me that some people go their whole lives never understanding the power of their voice. But when you grow up your entire life thinking you're inadequate, you run the risk of never truly understanding the power that your voice truly holds.

Sadly, at age 46, that was the story of my life. After supporting and sending my husband to college, I decided to go to college. I found myself standing wide-eyed in front of a group of 20-year-old college students in a state of absolute terror and panic.

Now, I don't know if you've ever experienced a stage fright attack, but I can tell you it is not pretty. My voice was trembling. I was nauseated. I just wanted to die. My voice was shaking horribly. "My n-name is L-Linda. The name of my C-company is..." As I looked into the audience, their eyeballs just got bigger and bigger the longer I spoke. I remember praying to God, "Please, just let me die."

When it was all over, the instructor asked me to stay after class. I told her, "You don't have to tell me. I know I made an F." I was shocked when she gave me an A for having the courage to complete the presentation.

Once I got home, I ran into the den, sat in my husband Don's lap and just sobbed. For five or ten minutes, I just cried and cried. But I took that experience and said to myself, "Okay, I have a problem. I need to learn how to do better."

So, that's what I did. I went to the highest level in college with speech communication. Then, I did Toastmasters. (Back then, you had to pay a penny every time you said an "um". Now, it's a nickel.) That stopped me from saying "um," "um," "um" every time I spoke.

I was doing anything and everything I could to improve. But despite all the practice, I still hadn't discovered my "kingpin" or limiting belief that was holding me back.

Now, I didn't grow up in poverty, and I wasn't physically abused. But I did grow up with an alcoholic father who ignored me. Heck, it wasn't until 30 seconds before he went into a coma (after struggling with a fatal bout of throat cancer) that he told me he loved me.

As this dying man held my hand and said, "Linda, I love you," all I could think to myself was, "You wait your whole life for your father to tell you that he loves you, and then he has to go and die."

It's a pretty stinkin' way to live. But at 17, I married a man who was the complete opposite of my father. He talked to me all the time and told me what he liked about me (and sometimes what he didn't.)

Do you think that was enough for me to believe I was good enough? No way! You see, Don was college educated, and I wasn't. So, I was still plagued with thoughts like, *I'm inadequate. I'm not good enough.* And once you step onto that *Crazy Train*, it becomes a vicious cycle with no emergency brake and no exit signs in sight.

There I was at 46 still feeling like I wasn't good enough. I became a workaholic to prove I wasn't dumb and that I wasn't a failure.

But two weeks into a Human Resources position at a local hospital's compensation department, I realized I had made the biggest mistake of my life. Every night, I would wake up feeling like there was an 800-pound elephant on my chest. I thought to myself, "Linda, this is it. You're dying."

So, I confided in a trusted friend, an RN, what was happening to me. She said, "Linda, you need to learn how to practice self-hypnosis." Now, I thought the whole self-hypnosis thing was a little woo-woo. But I was out of options, so I went.

Sitting in this "crazy" hypnotist's chair, I heard every word he said. "Linda, you're a fool," I thought. He gave me messages that I was self-confident, that I had self-esteem that I could do anything I wanted; that I was loved, that I was needed. I listened, but all the while was telling myself, "This is never going to work."

But when you're in a natural state of hypnosis, your inner critic (or the Tasmanian Devil as I call him) gets bored. Instead of rejecting those positive, affirming messages (like your Tasmanian Devil would do), your subconscious mind accepts them.

Then my life really changed. I realized I had more self-confidence, more self-esteem. I was just beginning to tap into the universal laws of the mind.

By 1993, after spending 17 years in Human Resources, I had given up that high-paying director's job, a month's vacation and great benefits to teach people what I had learned: *the universal laws of the mind.*

I quickly learned that you can be the best hypnotist in the world, but if no one knows about you, you will starve to death. You see, the fastest way to CASH in any business is to either double your rates or speak. So, I spoke. Any and every opportunity I had to speak, I took. Baton Rouge, New Orleans, Lafayette, San Antonio, I went anywhere and everywhere. I spoke. I spoke. I spoke.

In 1996, when I first started, I was making $4,000 total revenues per month. By the time I sold my business in 1999 to join Don after he retired, I was making $60,000 per month. I had set out to be the best weight-loss expert in the world, and I had succeeded.

Fast forward 15 years, and I was the author of the book, *Answering the Call*, which I co-authored with my friend and mentor, Lisa Sasevich. After the book became an instant #1 Best-Seller on Amazon, I was invited to speak to a crowd of hundreds of experts and entrepreneurs at the Annual Best-Seller's Summit in Hollywood, California!

It was such an honor to get to share my journey, my message and my mission with my fellow Best-Selling Authors®. But after the initial excitement, a little alarm went off in my head and reminded me that my absolute biggest fear was speaking from a stage to a room full of people!

But this wasn't my first rodeo. I had conquered this self-limiting belief before, and I was dead set on not letting it get the best of me again. So, I asked myself this question: *Was I going to let my fear hold me back, or was I going to take a deep breath, brush fear to the side and take this opportunity to do something that I believed in?*

When I wrapped up my speech, the response was unbelievable! I'm not exaggerating when I say that my fellow authors mobbed toward me, rushing the stage because they each wanted to talk about something I'd said, ask me a question or just give me a hug. I couldn't believe all of the love that a room full of strangers was willing to give to this little girl from Baton Rouge!

When the crowd finally cleared, JW Dicks, Co-Founder of The National Academy of Best-Selling Authors, leaned over to me and said, "This is what you're meant to do."

"He's right," I thought to myself. "This is why God put me through all of the pain I've been through in this life. This is my purpose and my passion—helping spread the word about how anyone can change their life without drugs and pills."

Now, I have spoken to audiences across the United States, everywhere from Palm Beach, Florida, to Hollywood, California. Just recently, I was invited to speak at a Level Up Conference in Tallahassee for Women's Prosperity Network. Thanks to the transformational work I have done in my mind, I was able to sell five figures from the stage-just from speaking to a live audience! Can you believe it?

Now, it's one thing to speak in front of an audience. It's quite another to speak in a way that helps people understand your message and buy into your offer. But that's exactly what I was able to do at Women's Prosperity Network's Level Up. It was such a thrill to see people rushing to the back of the room to buy my products and sign up for my programs! It was truly an amazing feat.

Now, with every speaking engagement or presentation I give, I'm widening my reach and impact. I'm helping people to *know* me, *like* me and *trust* me so they will want to do business with me and create this same type of transformation in their own lives.

It has been such a wild, exciting and beautiful ride! And as I have discovered the power and strength of my own voice, I am blessed to say that I have helped thousands of others do the same!

"When you're inspired you're not tired."
~ Nancy Matthews

Linda DeMarco,

CEO of Linda DeMarco Coaching, really has lived an amazing life - training, speaking, and teaching all over the world. A native of Connecticut, she holds her Bachelor's degree in Business, has her Certification from the Coaches Training Institute, and is also a Certified Yoga Instructor. A natural entrepreneur, Linda has built and developed a wide spectrum of businesses through the years, from importing to training. She has lived in Europe and Asia and currently resides in Florida, where she moved several years ago to be closer to her family and spoil her grandchildren.

You can contact Linda at:
(850) 273-1015
linda_demarco@comcast.net
www.lindademarco.com

Jump!

Linda DeMarco

"Whatever you can do or dream you can, begin it.
Boldness has genius, power, and magic in it!"
~ Goethe

You know, life is funny. What our expectations are and what our reality is ... well, they sometimes don't get the memo about where they should be at any given time. A lifetime ago, as a young woman just out of school, I landed what I thought was a dream job. It was in Human Resources, but rather than handle drama in an office, I had the chance to go speak to young men and women about job opportunities within the corporation I was working for. The biggest problem? I had to do a tremendous amount of public speaking with no real experience. Since I was never one to back down from a challenge, I accepted the position and simply joined Toastmasters. What better place to learn, right?

That was about the same time that I realized that public speaking is a little like cutting hair ... it's a lot harder than it looks. My first chance to speak at Toastmasters resulted in my hyperventilating, nearly passing out, and the pounding of my heart in my throat was, I'm sure, audible to most of the folks who witnessed that fiasco. It was a meltdown and a call to action all in one. I immersed myself in building myself. The vacations and new cars that my friends and coworkers were buying looked a lot better than taking Dale Carnegie – I did two rounds of that – but where they now have yellowing pictures, I have invested in me.

Fast forward to the present. I have built companies and trained people around the country, lived abroad for years at a time, and now move just as easily from a single conversation to engaging a crowd of 500. What changed?

Life. Mindset. Having your eyes and heart open to possibility. As Joseph Campbell says, "Jump!" That is easily one of my favorite quotes, and not just because it's easy to remember. That mindset of being in the moment, of being able to take action – *right then* – because you are prepared, has helped to drive my success that was the inspiration for me to continue to grow and help others.

My journey to the stage has been one of choosing to engage. I have had ups and downs in life and business, just like you. For many years, I trained men and women in businesses I was building or those that I worked for; and, in the end, I realized that everybody, no matter how competent, sometimes needs a push. My training experience grew into the chance to teach English abroad in South Korea and France, and I enjoyed it immensely. As my career grew and branched out, opportunities for speaking grew. Where did these chances come from? I simply said yes. The amazing life has followed.

I turned all that teaching and training experience into a coaching business ... by accident. Long before it was fashionable, I started my coaching career through the Coaches Training Institute because, to me, coaching, teaching, and training are all shade from the same tree. The intention? Become better at training and teaching. The result? Coaching gave me a feeling of satisfaction beyond anything I had ever gotten from training someone for a business. In the business world, as a trainer and teacher, you do love to see people you have brought on become better and better. Knowing that you helped someone become more competent in his or her career, simply put, feels good.

Helping others to take a step in life? Seeing and hearing the elation in their voices as they talk about a change you helped to make possible? That feels *great.*

One of my favorite examples is from my years in Paris. I had said yes (see a trend forming here?) and had the chance to live and teach in France. In the course of my time there, I spoke to a variety of groups and had been invited, as a coach, to give a lecture to a women's group about "What's Possible" when you hire a coach. After the talk, a young lady had stayed behind to ask me about life coaching.

Stacy loved the French culture, spoke the language beautifully, and had, for years, dreamed of living in France. To make matters worse, she even had a French last name. She was, literally, reminded of her goal at every turn. She had loads of desire to move her home to France; she just didn't have the confidence to take the leap.

And what a big leap it would be! Job, home, family! For us in the United States, the idea of simply moving to a new house is daunting, but another country? It can be a paralyzing decision and that was exactly what it had done to her.

I agreed to meet Stacy at an outdoor café overlooking the Seine; of course, the very picture many of us hold for Paris. As we talked in the warm spring sunshine, she shared her ideas, her goals, and her dreams. I could clearly hear in her voice the longing and passion she had for this idea, as well as the trepidation about how she could possibly do it. Up until that moment, she had no idea how she could ever realize her dreams, and finally, I simply asked her, "Why not say yes to this dream?"

She didn't have an answer.

Over the following months, I was able to work with Stacy and help her plan her move to Paris. She lived there for the next four years before returning to the United States, and, simply put, she was able to live the dream. Not "if only" or "what if", but "*I did.*"

That's why I choose to be a life coach and a speaker. For me, of course, the two go hand in hand. I help people engage in and live their dreams whether it be in a life path or on a career path. Nothing is as fulfilling as reaching out to an audience of 500 people and causing them to ask themselves, "Why *not* say yes?"

A great case in point, I was giving a lecture on procrastination and the light bulb went on for a doctor named Tim. He came, he listened, and he realized that his dream of taking off for six months to travel was never going to happen without a push. During the course of our conversations, I was able to push Tim off the fence and get him moving. We worked through several strategy sessions and he understood that he *could* take the time, he *could* travel abroad. His life changed, his values changed, and he found his passion. Finally, he was clear on what really mattered in life, and he was able to make that the focal point of his life instead of a bullet point.

I look back on my own amazing life: the sense of empowerment that my philosophy of saying yes has given me, and the amazing chances to impact *lives,* not just careers. Coaching and speaking have opened doors for me to reach out and grant people the wishes they have by showing them the steps to take to reach those goals. My journey *to* the stage has really been more of a journey *through* the stage. Speaking is a part of my life *because* of my life, and as a result, I change lives. I can think of no more noble task, nor one so rewarding, as the help I give people. So remember – JUMP!

Paulina Lopez,

CPC, CBC, is a life and business coach who empowers ambitious and passionate women with clarity and confidence for personal and professional success.

She works with you to begin your transformation with building a solid foundation, by your own definition, through self-awareness and inspired action! You'll work together on creating systems and structures, strengthening your wealth consciousness and breaking free of your money story. She'll push you forward (lovingly), teach you to set boundaries and hold you accountable while supporting you every step of the way. As you experience greater results, you'll cultivate and embrace a level of mastery, living the life you desire. Wealth and success isn't just about the pursuit of making money, it's about who YOU become in the process. Know that YOU are your greatest asset... and the best investment you can make is in yourself!

Contact Paulina at www.paulinalopezcoaching.com.

Awaken Your Impact: Deliver Value | Inspire Change | Empower Others

Paulina Lopez

The Beginning Journey to the Stage

The first time I spoke in public, I was terrified! The thought of having a room full of people staring at me and possibly judging me was intimidating! Growing up, I was shy in school. I was afraid to raise my hand in class, even though I knew the answers. In the third grade, we began reading our stories and essays out loud. I was so nervous waiting for my name to be called to speak in front of the class. But once it was over, my teacher praised my story telling and voice projection, and I wanted to do it over and over again!

As a child, I went to acting and dance classes. My mother noticed a spark in me at a very young age that I had not yet recognized in myself. By the time I was in middle school, I expanded into ballroom dancing and hip hop. At a time when most kids experience their awkward stages in puberty, I experienced my metamorphosis. My dance teacher took me under her wing, and I had the opportunity to be part of every school performance in the 7th and 8th grades. I was honored with a performance art award. I discovered dance to be a form of art and excelled in my creative nature. It was exhilarating to be on stage and my confidence level and self-esteem skyrocketed.

Change for the Better

My professional background is in finance and human resources. Both gave me valuable experience.

Finance gave me the systems, structures and organization to be a quick thinker and problem solver. Human resources taught me so much about people and relationships; but it's what I've studied and learned about mindset and transformation that has helped me to identify thought process and behavioral patterns. I'm grateful for my career experiences, yet I knew I was settling, playing small—playing it safe. I was dealing with self-doubt and insecurity. My true calling is to create an emotional connection with others on a compassionate level, being of service, supporting and providing maximum value and advancement. I want to have a massive positive impact in the WORLD.

But like everyone seeking to fulfill their purpose, I needed to experience my own reflection and self-realization. Even our greatest leaders had to go through their own reflection before communicating their vision to change the world! For the past ten years, I have been on my journey of returning to who I AM at the innermost core. This journey has allowed me to embrace my uniqueness and live a life of authenticity and integrity. In 2007 I felt the shift...a deep desire for change, a feeling of purpose. I realized I needed to fully invest in myself personally and professionally. With the support of mentors and healers, and by reading books and attending workshops, my life has transformed into an amazing journey, affecting both my personal and professional development. It has awakened me to my purpose as a facilitator. Because of this profound impact, I became passionate about empowerment, which is what led to becoming certified as a life coach and professional business coach.

Stepping Up to the Stage

Coaching has allowed me to realize my childhood dream of becoming a teacher, a facilitator! For the first time, I was presenting who I knew myself to be and what I was truly meant to do. I knew speaking would provide a platform for me to share my vision, mission and passion. In the beginning, most entrepreneurs tend to hide behind their computers and mistake being busy with being productive, when the most important thing is to get out and build strong, solid and lasting relationships! Like most entrepreneurs, my response to spending and investing in my business at the beginning stages was usually a NO! Yet I knew I was ready to claim my place as an empowered feminine leader!

The turning point came when I made the bold and courageous decision to begin the journey of public speaking. I knew that this was something I had to master. The first time I had the opportunity to present myself and my business, it wasn't good! I was upset with myself for not being able to engage the audience, delivering content and value, without being in my head. The second time I was approached to speak, I was better prepared. I put aside the feelings of fear by doing it anyway, stepping through it and being in the moment. I spoke slowly, from the heart, and made sure to connect with my audience. My confidence level shifted when I approached it with a purpose.

When there's a confidence and certainty about YOU, people are influenced by what you're communicating to them. AND people will naturally be drawn to you! The power you have to influence the results you desire is in the energy and confidence YOU exude! Something *has* to resonate with your audience, and it has to be within YOU!

Growth and Transformation

Speaking has been instrumental for my personal and professional development and awakened me to my purpose. I now have a burning desire to inspire and empower others to achieve greatness in their lives. When I began coaching, I thought the biggest obstacle I would face with business owners was a lack of sales and revenue. But I discovered the real obstacles are a lack of self-worth, confidence and clarity; a feeling of inadequacy; and the need to stay motivated to succeed. Overcoming these obstacles is the true success!

I am committed to becoming better at helping others transform their lives, which is why I continue to learn, grow and invest in myself! YOU are your greatest asset. The best investment you can make is in yourself! True entrepreneurship is inspiring the world to be better and sharing your passion with the world. And if you're in business to help others, you can't help them until they give themselves permission to say YES! And they won't say YES to themselves until they know YOU can empower them! That starts with your power to facilitate the results they desire! Your energy and presence MUST be filled with confidence, clarity, and certainty!

Inspiration and Motivation to Take the Stage and Speak

When I observed the energy of someone I admired on stage, I'd be mesmerized with their presence. Their ability to fully connect with their audience, the movement of their hands, the genuine smiles and contagious laughter, the pauses and the vibration of their voice, and their energy! I saw that they approached conversation with no hidden agenda and no hidden motive. It all seemed to come naturally to them. I wanted that! What I've learned from watching those on stage that truly resonates with me is the way they made the audience feel that they were speaking directly to them! Speaking to an audience is about having a conversation. It's about connecting to them authentically, from the heart, to give them an experience!

I believe the most important attribute one gains in speaking is...*confidence*! Confidence is what attracts others to you and to be intrigued by YOU! Sometimes it's not about what you say, your service or products, the amazing work you do or the credentials that you've amassed. It's about who you are BE-ing! Your presence, that "spark" you exude, your magnetism and the confidence you possess!

A message that has transformed the way I approach speaking is in the book *The Power of Now* by Eckhart Tolle. His message is to not get stuck in the past or worry about the future but to live in the Now! The present moment is all we ever have! This helped me tremendously in silencing my thoughts and being in my stillness.

Finding Your Voice for Your Journey to the Stage

As business owners, executives and career professionals, we have the stage as a platform to express our ideas, our missions and our visions. To build trust and establish credibility, it's important to focus on contribution, creativity and collaboration. Don't focus on competition; there's no such thing as a lack of opportunities. The best way to cultivate credibility authentically is by projecting what's on the inside, your signature and your authentic voice! It's the magnetism that draws others to you. You don't need to be everything to everyone. Be honest and stay true to your core values to represent yourself with integrity. Understanding how to craft a message that prompts people to take inspired action is a skill every organization and entrepreneur needs!

Having this level of unstoppable dedication to creating the business and life you want is what truly determines your success. Develop a clear and compelling picture of the message you want to deliver to your audience. Commit to bringing forth the strong, confident person you desire to be! Speaking in front of an audience may seem challenging, yet it's actually an exciting and rewarding experience! This is your chance to be an inspirer, an expert, an influencer, an authentic leader!

*"Success is available to anyone willing to give it their all.
Great success however, is only possible through the magic of
collaboration and partnership with others."*
~ Trish Carr

Ana Atibet

is a Certified Speaker, published author, Women's Prosperity Network Chapter Leader in Broward County (FL), a leader in the South Florida Latin Community, "Mompreneur," a Multi-Organizational Networking Happy Hours Facilitator, Certified Wedding Planner, Fashion Designer, and Graphic Designer. She is the proud owner of *BF Cake Lollipop Inc.*, a company specializing in chocolates, candy buffets, and special events. As a Mompreneur, Ana loves to inspire and empower women on their journeys through life and business.

You can contact Ana at:
BFcakeLollipop@gmail.com
www.BFcakeLollipop.com
You can also find her on Social Media: Facebook, Twitter, LinkedIn, and Instagram.

From Mom to Entrepreneur "Mompreneur" ~ From Hobby to Money

Ana Atibet

Once upon a time there was a little girl who dreamed of being on stage as a Fashion Designer and being recognized wherever she went. She wanted to inspire other kids to believe in themselves and to display their unique talents. She was so energetic and creative, and with the support of her family, she was unstoppable. She sang in a church chorus, was president of various clubs, designed and made her own clothes, loved to dance, and wrote poems. She enjoyed every single moment with friends and family.

At the age of 16, she got her first real job as an atelier in her small town in Puerto Rico and got to design all the prom dresses for her friends. Life was *perfect* until her joint pain started bothering her again and she had to see a rheumatoid arthritis specialist. Every single day she cried, because of her pain and all the medication, especially the cortisone and its side effects. The worst part was realizing she couldn't go to New York City to follow her dreams to become an international fashion designer, because of the cold weather and her need to continue her treatments.

For the first time, she felt like crap as her dreams seemed to vanish before her. Still, she was not willing to stop dreaming, and she waited for a miracle as she put all of her faith in God's hands and trusted that everything was happening for a reason.

Her marketing teacher asked her what her dreams were, and she said, "To be a fashion designer and to inspire others, but I can't," she said, and she then explained why. The teacher, seeing her passion and desire, believed in her and her talents so much that she researched all of the fashion schools in the United States and found one in Miami, Florida, where the weather was similar to that in Puerto Rico.

After the teacher submitted the application, representatives from the school traveled to the island to meet the talented young lady and to talk with her parents. Much to her delight, she was accepted. Woohoo!

The next few years were a whirlwind. She moved to Florida. After graduation, she got to travel and work with different artists, and then she married. She created costumes for a movie and became the head designer at Gables Couture.

The end...not really. That little girl (that is still living inside me) became the woman that I am now, having the same burning desires.

From Mom to Entrepreneur

To be honest, I was so happy, clueless, and very young. When I had my daughter, my precious angel, I realized how fast my life had changed. She had to stay in intensive care for eight days and that experience was worse than any of the joint pain I had as a teenager. Then at five months old, she was back in intensive care with a weird case of Kawasaki Disease.

What choice did I have? I decided to put my career on hold, so I could be fully present and raise my little angel. Before this I had everything I had dreamed of and worked for, and now I had to figure out how to make money from home, because my husband couldn't pay for everything.

I started studying graphic design and began selling beauty products to help pay the bills. Soon I was earning prizes with the beauty company, and as my team grew to more than 44 consultants, I started earning a nice income.

Then, I decided to have another baby. During my first month of pregnancy, I started bleeding and they put me on bed rest until the last month. This was another unexpected challenge and this time I had to think about myself, my health, and being confined to bed, if I wanted to have a healthy baby boy.

It was the longest eight months ever! Thankfully, my son was full term; however, he had to stay in intensive care. This shifted my priorities again. My kids were my life now, my new dream and reality.

When I Got Lost

I was preoccupied with diapers, kids playing in the park, household chores, homework, and helping friends with their own problems and business challenges. Then, my father died. At that moment I realized I was completely EMPTY. I did not know who I was anymore, and I believed if I started thinking about what I wanted, I was being selfish.

A year later, when my BFF was having a baby shower, I went back to Puerto Rico to support her and see my family. While there I decided to stop by a local chocolate store to pick up some chocolate-covered strawberries for my aunt. The store had just opened and the gentleman was very kind, explaining I would have to wait for the chocolate to melt so he could prepare my strawberries.

As the chocolate melted, we had an awesome conversation. He told me his story and how he ended up having his store. Then he asked me, "Why don't you do this in Miami? You obviously love chocolate." Then, it became obvious to me that my visit to his store was no coincidence — it was meant to be!

In a free class, the store owner taught me what to do, gave me his list of suppliers, and inspired me to create my own chocolates. What could be more perfect? Now, I had something new and sweet to give to my family and friends.

I soon became obsessed with the world of chocolate. I started with practicing with recipes, reading blogs, and sharing my chocolates with others — and they absolutely loved them!

I never stopped to think, *"Oh, no, I don't know how to do it,"* or *"I'm not good enough."* I just saw an opportunity to express my creativity, joy, and love to others, *and* do it part-time at home. I LOVED being my own boss and as my business grew, it evolved from chocolates to Cake Pops. My company, *Best Friends Cake Lollipop, Inc.,* offers more than 27 flavors that are "the best way to enjoy cake!" Soon my perfect hobby started making a little money.

On My Own

After 18 years I didn't expect to find myself separated, a single mom with two kids suffering from ADHD, asthma, and allergies. Most of my friends lived far away. I had no real income. I cried alone for so many nights, not knowing where my family's next meal would come from and watching my credit score plunge as I maxed out my credit cards. The despair grew as I sought support from federal agencies to cover my children's medical expenses. I asked my mother and friends for money to support my dreams, while working hard to make them a reality. Still, you know what? I am proud that I did what I had to do. I never stopped believing. I've always had faith and I prayed every single day. I have been grateful for everything, because I knew "all this, too, shall pass."

From Hobby to Money

I had no time to cry, because the bills were piling up fast, so I started doing expos and bazaars to find new customers for my chocolates.

Soon I found one key to my future success. As Oprah says, "Surround yourself with people who take you higher." Besides networking, I decided to check out Women's Prosperity Network (WPN), and from that moment on my life changed forever. I no longer felt alone, because these women are so *totally freaking awesome*! They support me and my business. They believe in *me* and show me how I can support others. And, for all of this I am truly thankful to the founding sisters and members of WPN.

I became a WPN Chapter Leader to support other women who are going through challenges similar to mine. At one time I was ashamed to tell someone my story, and today I know it is necessary. This is how I overcome my fears and obstacles in life. What matters most is being authentic and having an open heart. To love and be loved, to help and accept help, and knowing it's all going to be okay.

Getting lost was the only way I found myself. I never wait for the right moment to jump. I just do it! I have faith and I follow my heart. My mother always tells me, "When you already have the *No*, you go after the *Yes*."

Whatever you are going through right now is just temporary. You are the only one who can choose to see what you are going through as problems or opportunities. Talk to positive people and avoid negative ones. Never think you are better than others. Compete only with yourself. Listen to and support others and their dreams. Ask for what you need. BE YOURSELF and BE PRESENT. We always have angels in our lives. It's time to open your hands to start receiving and be sure to ALWAYS SMILE.

This is my Journey to the Stage. Now, how can I support you?

"Life's journey is long. Be sure to take along some great friends (and some good snacks too!)"
~ Nancy Matthews

Revella Carter Hadley

is President and CEO of Black Swan Special Events, and is a native Floridian. As president of the company, she decided to carry on her father's tradition of providing great food to the community. Her father was known in the Ft. Lauderdale community for his restaurant's namesake of Chuck's 00-Soul. His specialty was his trademark and tasteful ribs, a recipe he passed down to his daughter. Revella is a graduate of Leadership of North Broward as well as the Jim Moran Institute for Global Entrepreneurship. The company continues to expand its operations in the growing industry of event planning, catering, and entertainment services.

You can contact Revella at:
(954) 529-5962
rhadley@blackswanspecialevents.com
www.blackswanspecialevents.com

My Training Ground

Revella Hadley

My early speaker training started with my performing Easter and Christmas speeches at church.

Later came cheerleading and drill team. So, I've always been comfortable in front of an audience. In those days, I would practice saying the words in the mirror and then do a sort of pre-show for my parents. This was my way of working through some of the little kinks prior to rehearsal.

I used this same method with my four kids, but it didn't always work. On one occasion my middle son, who was about four years old at the time, had a simple, two-line Christmas speech. He had done so well at home, as well as in rehearsal. As the entire family sat in anticipation, he stepped to the front, saw the crowd, and not one word came out! I stepped into the aisle so he could see me. I offered up my best "Do it for mommy." Not a sound. He just stood there with tears streaming down those big brown eyes and stared. After a few more seconds that seemed like an eternity, he ran and buried his head in my lap.

The stage can take on many forms.

I am a caterer by trade. My "stage" often comes in the form of trade shows and festivals. My signature product is bar-b-q ribs. I am developing a plan to market them nationally.

I do these as a part of my marketing piece and it helps me create my stage experience. One type of presentation I do is at

Home shows. A trade show can be considered a stage because you are interacting with people and sharing your knowledge of a product or service. This is also a great time to work on eye contact.

During the presentation, I explain how the recipe was passed down from my dad. I then talk about the dry rub process, and the minimum four-hour marinating time. As I'm demonstrating the technique, I'm looking directly at them. If it's an outdoor event, I show the grill and the flames. I remove the slab from the grill. As the slab sizzles on the chopping block, the cleaver comes down and divides each bone from the next. I then drizzle the rib with bar-b-q sauce and gently place in the hands of a hungry guest. As they take the first bite, it's all smiles.

My words showed the guests my knowledge of the product and my actions made them want to try a sample.

Each time I step on stage I get such a high.

I married Derrick, an incredible guy with an awesome singing voice. He decided to form his own singing group. From time to time he would have performers who weren't available for one reason or another. One day I said to him jokingly, "You know that I know all the steps."

He responded, "Let's do it." At the ripe "young" age of 47, I became a backup singer.

I still remember the first time I stepped on stage as a backup singer. As the curtain opened, and the music started, I felt as though everyone was looking at me. I was so excited. I remembered my steps, and I remembered my verses. It was a 90-minute choreographed show, but time seemed to go by so quickly. All the hours of rehearsal, the wardrobe fittings, everything came down to this moment, and I loved it!

Since my first experience, our group has opened for First Lady Michele Obama, as well as for the Grammy-award winning group, the Spinners. I have worked with many truly amazing singers. The one thing I notice about each of them is that no matter what may be going on in their personal lives, it all gets put on hold when they step on stage. Making your presentation your total focus helps you give the audience your best.

My final thoughts: In my Journey to the stage I have found that knowing your subject matter is the most significant point. Look at your time on stage as an opportunity to share what you are passionate about. When you are confident about your message, you can be more creative with your delivery.

Stephanie Pimental

lives the story of her success. Growing up in a broken home, being in foster care and on food stamps, she learned the hard way. Yet, she educated herself and fought her way back. This led her to create Extraordinary Visions and Extraordinary Money Making Kids, teaching financial education.

The best part is that Stephanie has not forgotten where she came from. Her website, www.extraordinaryvisions.org, offers education, strategy sessions, and programs while providing scholarships to those who are most at risk. Stephanie acts as a Guardian Ad Litem for the State of Florida. (http://guardianadlitem.org/) She is a Licensed Life, Annuities and Securities Representative in Florida.

You can connect with Stephanie at:
(561) 632-8735
Stephanie@extraordinaryvisions.org

From Food Stamps and Foster Care to Financial Freedom

Stephanie Pimental

I have been called the credit lady, the money lady, and the game lady, but that is not how I started out.

Like many children, I was never given any real education about money. I grew up in a broken home, and food stamps and foster care did little to teach me anything about how to manage money when it was around. Growing up in an abusive home did little for my confidence, and moving around every two years made sure I didn't have friends or support.

I can say self-confidence has been a huge challenge. It is a challenge for everyone in some way. Know that if you keep believing and striving towards your desire, no matter what it is, you can achieve it! My only desire when I was younger was to be better and have a better life than the one I was living. Being brought up in an abusive home, I often got a sense that something wasn't right but did not realize it until someone told me that there was something better.

My first memory of being on stage was when I was six years old. I was in a very small town in North Carolina. My school had all the grades, 1st through 12th. The 12th graders loved me. They thought I was cute and made me their mascot. I would attend their school events whenever my mom let me. There was a senior event where I had to stand on stage and speak to the audience. I remember being so excited and so anxious to go up there and show them what I could do. I had the cutest blue dress on and my hair looked pretty. One thing I guess no one thought of was to have me to go to the bathroom before I went on stage. I got up there and was so excited that, when I was supposed to speak, all I could do was cry and say, "I have to go to the bathroom," as I peed my pants right on stage! Well, as you can imagine, I was totally embarrassed, and of course everyone laughed. That was my first experience of being on stage!

I was removed from my home at the age of 13. It was a challenging time for me. I was angry, and drugs and alcohol were easy solutions to mask the pain, if I could get my hands on them. Throughout my life, there was a recurring theme of using drugs and alcohol to mask my feelings. It has only been recently that I have been able to face my feelings and thoughts and not hide in substance abuse. I had to stay in a group home for a while, and after that, my great aunt agreed to be my Guardian and take care of me. I was labeled as a troubled teen. My great aunt decided to enroll me in a private school. She and I discussed finding my biological father, so we contacted my grandparents and told them the situation and what we were trying to do. Remember, having a child come from an abusive home was embarrassing for everyone, especially since they all felt they should have known what was going on and should have done something.

We contacted my father, and he flew out to see me right away! He was not sure how to handle the situation, as he was married and had a young daughter. So I went to visit him on spring break and was introduced to my stepmom and stepsister. My sister, who was only 5 at the time, was happy to have a bigger sister. I was still angry and dealing with my own issues, so it took some time for the two of us to really become sisters.

Later, I moved to Colorado to live with my father and his family. We went through years of therapy and trials and tribulations due to my rebelling, but we made it through. My stepmother is now one of my best friends.

I started living on my own when I was 17 years old. My father and stepmother had divorced. I had a series of different jobs including retail merchandising, government sales, contracting for supplies, property management, and working in a funeral home.

The stage started to call me about 15 years later. I was doing volunteer work for an educational company that had changed my life. I had spoken to my mother again after 15 years of no communication and me still holding a grudge. All this made a huge impact on my self-confidence. I had always been in the back of the room, playing a supportive role of volunteering. Then I was asked to do the company's training and be in the front of the room for a course appropriately named "Self-Expression and Leadership". I was really unsure about my ability to do it. The people around me were very supportive and had a huge amount of faith in me, so I went for it! The training was intense, and I had to do a lot of work on my insecurities and confidence issues! Being in front of the room was awesome and something I knew I was supposed to do!

I left the education company after two years and pursued a career in legal and finances, which led me to educate myself about all the negative things people were experiencing in finances--bankruptcy, foreclosures, short sales, collection issues, and credit issues. I went into this field because I knew I needed to learn about finances and credit, and I ended up filing for bankruptcy myself. I worked on behalf of the consumers and loved helping people.

Well, the stage started calling me again! Now it was to teach and educate others about credit for small groups inside the office, but it was enough! I also started volunteering as a Guardian Ad Litem and played money games with kids at Kids in Distress and worked in a program where teens in foster care were studying to get their GED. I found out I really loved doing this, and I gave the teens new ways to think about money and finances.

After 10 years, I left the law firm, got a divorce, and then my mother passed away. I was grateful that I had reconciled with her and had had the last 14 years of healing and new memories! And I stopped relying on drugs and alcohol. That continues to be such a huge blessing, and my clarity just kept getting better and better!

I now wondered what I was to do next. Where did I want to make a difference and who did I want to be? The funny thing is I kept seeing myself on stage, and I saw myself writing a book in which I would share my story and inspire others!

Today I am Founder of Extraordinary Visions "Smart Money Big Purpose" where we provide educational tools to help people get their money working for them and fulfill their big purpose in life, and Extraordinary Money Making Kids where we mentor teens in two courses: "Thriving Teens" financial education and "Youthrenuership".

I am so grateful to be with Women's Prosperity Network, a great group of women that support me and provide the resources for me to achieve my dreams and visions and to reach my goals. I am honored to be a part of this book, and my desire is that you are moved, touched, and inspired to follow the dreams and visions that are calling you!

Varsha Bhongade

was born and raised in Bombay, India, and, before immigrating to the United States in 1991, she graduated with a Bachelor's degree in Textiles from Nirmala Neketan College of Home Science, University of Bombay. Although she has been the president of Craig's Designs Inc. in Stuart, Florida, for over 17 years, she has found the time to stay in a committed relationship for the last 15. Despite all the distractions of a business, she still holds a commercial pilot's license. Though she swears that one day she will slow down enough to adopt a Black Lab.

You can contact Varsha at Varsha@craigsdesigns.com.

Rebel Without, er... *With* a Cause

Varsha Bhongade

Ever since I was asked to contribute to this book, I've been agonizing over what the hell I was going to write. My Journey to the Stage? Umm, yeah, right. I'll get right on it. What story could I possibly tell that will correlate?

As I thought about it, though, I realized that all my life, I have loved stories, whether they were the recollections of my mother of her childhood in the colony or from the scriptures my grandmother read in her daily worship rituals. A favorite that I remember was that of the queen scouring the countryside to look for clothing worn by happy women so she could also be happy. To me, it was an epiphany to see that the queen's happiness had nothing to do with her clothes and everything to do with her mindset. Happiness is a choice for all of us – when you stick to that path, acceptance of the choice becomes your compass.

As I reflected on it, though, I realized, my life *has* been about journeys and many of those journeys resulted in helping people. I grew up in India, the youngest of four children. As such, I think I was afforded a lot more autonomy than my siblings ... maybe because my parents thought I was special, maybe just because they had relaxed a little, having already raised three other children. In either case, I figured it out and as I look back on those years, I realize that I have always thought differently without *deciding* to be different. Standing up for others came easily; if I saw a wrong, I wanted to help right it. I wanted to remind people that what is *right* is *real*.

In my life, it is simply my blessing that has driven my desire to speak out. As a child and a young woman in India, I was compelled to speak out for the underdog, to defend those who needed it. The funny thing to think about, now, is that I was just a puny kid then, in some cases fighting to defend those bigger and older than me who were in trouble. For about a two-year period, I swear I couldn't see my knees; they wore scabs from all the fights and scraps I got into defending the proverbial "underdog". Our family doctor nicknamed me "The Rebel" and I'm sure he tired of seeing me so often.

Now, years later as a woman in America, the irony is that I have been blessed to surround myself with so many like-minded men and women that I no longer actively see the help I provide to people – from the stage or from the office, it is always right there for the giving, rolling off my tongue. Of course, every once in a while, I catch a glimpse of it, but so many of my close friends and business confidants have such a wonderful servant's mentality that I no longer see "help" or "advice" as an active choice. It is as natural as the sun on the leaves. For me to not help someone would be impossible. The catch to that? Many times, my advice, given freely, so obvious to me, hurts because the listener simply made the problem. I cannot count the times I see that the issue or problem that people have is a rut that only *they* perceive. Why does that drive me crazy? *They aren't ruts!* People slow down or start over, thinking nothing and when they do, BAM! Forward motion stops and the struggle against nothing starts. I continually find myself asking people, as a speaker and a mentor, "If you know what to do, and you know why you're not doing it, how can anybody else help you? Do what you know is right for you and the business, and the problem will be gone."

That is the role I play now, that of the rebel *with* a cause. I still see myself as a protector of people, but now, instead of protecting them from the bully on the playground or the street, I protect them from the negativity and second-guessing they face in their own mind. I use my presence and expertise as a speaker to effect change in others. The words and wisdom that I share help people to work through their challenges, be it in business or in life or that shady grey area where those two all too often intersect. And that is where I always get in trouble and one of the reasons that I choose to elevate my speaking presence. Some folks just need a good verbal slap. Paralysis by analysis sets in, and they get lost in minutia. A real friend, or a really good speaker, can draw them back to the reality they left and remind them of their duty and job ... making money and a livelihood. More than that, making a life and a career.

Okay, time for *my* dirty little secret ... without being vain, I can say that I have never struggled to make money. Yeah, right? Yeah, really. I have built businesses, bought businesses, and grown businesses. Have I lost battles along the way? Of course. Have I won the war? Yes. How I did that is not important; what is most important is that I know I can share with people how they can win their battles and wars. I'm in the clothing business, and after many years of doing it, I just see things in terms of t-shirts. "I need to paint the house? Okay, that's three orders. Let's make some calls and get it done."

Too many times I see people thinking too hard about the simple process of making money. They ascribe some magical power to their business, as though it was a sacred gift instead of a sacred duty, so the idea to quantify it in terms of dollars, to them, somehow cheapens it. To that I say, "If the horse makes friends with the hay, what is it going to eat?" This is your business! Make it work for you, not the other way around.

Money? You have a business; go make the money you need. Family? Bring the people into the business that will allow you the time you need to be a mother, a wife, a husband, a father. Time? Manage yours better, as we all get the same amount each week. You can provide for yourself with no problem, so quit losing sleep, start moving, and you will see that your problems don't solve themselves; you solve them.

My journey to the stage has been one that has gone from defeating the "bully" outside in the street to defeating the "bully" inside my listeners' minds. As I have grown and matured, I see that so many of our *real* problems are those we make up in our own mind. Open yourself up to being real, and you will see that real answers are already in you. If not, call me, and I will tell you the same thing. I may slap you around for letting yourself get stuck in this mind trap, but I will help you get free…. and sell you a t-shirt for your troubles!

"Know, understand and believe that the why gets you high, the 'ing' is the thing and the how is the wow."
~ Susan Wiener

Jamie Gilleland

is the CEO and Founder of MiSyte.com, a digital marketing and sales automation company. She holds a Bachelor's in Information Technology, an MBA in Marketing and Management, and has coached, trained, and helped businesses of all sizes to impact their online presence. Jamie makes her home in Southeast Georgia with her children and fiancé, the writer Chris Groote. Additional members of the household include several spoiled cats and a neurotic Golden Retriever named Griz.

Contact information:
(843) 263-5478
jamie@misyte.com
www.misyte.com

A Butterfly's Journey

Jamie Gilleland

You want a sob story? I've got a great one. I could tell it to you and you'd think it was either a hoax or a reality television show. Ups, downs, ins and outs; they are all somewhere back there in my life.

Guess what? It's no different than your story. You've dealt with your problems; I've dealt with mine. Either way, it's all ancient history. The things that have happened to all of us may echo in our lives, but they no longer *control* our lives.

While those things may help define me, they do not inspire me. One day, and that day will come soon, I will sit down and write a book about all of those things and that history that helped to produce the woman I am today. That time is not now, though; there is too much abundance in life to worry about those things from the past.

I will tell you this - I took many years to figure out that, as much as I love my business, God and Fate did not keep me here to just build websites. My purpose is not to run a business, or be a Mom or a wife. It is to help. To inspire. To grow.

That same focus and drive that propelled my career in sales and the corporate world years ago *does* still define who I am, but my story is *now*, not years ago. My story is about *me*, not some corporate entity that needed a skill set, regardless of who carried it. That brings us to the really good stuff... where did my journey to this stage start, and how have I changed as a person since it began?

After a great sales run in the computer industry in the early nineties, I began to use that knowledge to train, and was a corporate level trainer in Wells Fargo's Home Mortgage Division. A huge part of that job was, of course, speaking to groups. Now, those groups started small, and as my career progressed, those audiences got larger and larger. Nervous? Yep. The shakes, the butterflies, you name it. I could always keep it together, but I was the face of an entire organization for my audience. I was CORPORATE... somehow, whenever people said that, I always felt it was implied that it was in all caps and almost derogatory. In the back of my mind, no matter the group, I always felt that people in the audience were not who they would normally be, either. They put on the face they wanted Wells Fargo to see; they were on their BEST BEHAVIOR. Remember how your mother would tell you to be on your BEST BEHAVIOR and you *knew* it was capitalized? Everybody in the room was looking for a gold star and nobody wanted to be, for want of a better term, "real".

I hated it and loved it at the same time. I was very good at what I did, but I was just an actress on the stage. Nervousness and doubts would always creep up, on butterfly wings, as though somebody in the audience was going to suddenly jump up and yell, "That's not the real Jamie Gilleland! Stone her!" As much as I enjoyed it, I was never comfortable in front of an audience. Enter Dr. Steven R. Covey.

(Some of you younger folks may not know just how much Covey's business philosophies impacted American companies in the 1990s. His *7 Habits of Highly Effective People* is still among the most-read books for entrepreneurs and business people. To say he had "rock star" status would be like saying that Mozart wrote some awfully snappy tunes.)

I had been teaching and training Covey's methods at Wells Fargo for quite a while and knew them inside and out. I could go on and on about *7 Habits* and, of course, when Wells Fargo hired Steven Covey to come speak at a corporate function, I got the nod to introduce him. Nervous? I worried that I was going to get carried off by the butterflies in my stomach. And then I was introduced to Steven Covey himself backstage.

Now, I'm not a shrinking violet, but here was the guy I was not only introducing, but whose systems I had been implementing and training for years. In a style that I'm convinced only he could pull off, he made small talk for a minute or two, and then politely asked if I was nervous. When I said that I was a little nervous (the understatement of the year), he smiled. Here was a man that I really respected, and I knew that Wells Fargo was paying him $75,000 to speak to a group of nearly 3,000 that day. And you know what? He looked at me and said, "When those butterflies go away before you start speaking, get out of the business, because you don't care anymore."

Now, nearly 20 years later, as a regular speaker in front of a myriad of business groups of almost any size, I think that he was right, but we were at two completely different levels of engagement in that passing conversation. The young lady he gave that advice to was just worried about screwing up in front of an audience. Today, the butterflies I get are nervousness that I won't be able to help the people that have come to listen to me.

What has caused that change in my mindset? Maturity? Experience? Judgment? Probably. More than likely, though, it is the fact that, when I take the stage or meet with my clients, it is as a vehicle for them, not me. I'm not here to sell them a website or a system; I'm here to *help* them. They realize that I can help them to build and grow a business, and I know that they really need help. Nervous? Very. Butterflies? Yep. The livelihood of these people is in my hands, they trust me. If I don't nurture that, they fail. If my words and actions don't ring true or somehow I don't communicate the message, their company does not have the growth I know it can.

At the same time, the people listening to me have changed, too. They aren't there because they were told to go by some middle manager, because drinks and snacks would be provided, or they get to leave work early to go to an off-site meeting. My audience has become "real" people. They are trying to become better for the sake of their businesses and their lives, so, unlike my audiences at Wells Fargo, they are committed to listening and growing.

As I have grown as a businesswoman and a speaker, I have come to realize that anybody can get to this next level. How? Passion! Don't confuse the nervousness for the task with nervousness for the job! Understand that you have a great responsibility to your listeners that is so much more than whether your choice of words is "right" or "correct". You simply must believe that the critics and the cynics in your audience do not understand the value of *anything*, therefore, their opinion of your message or offer has no bearing. Your job, as a speaker or a business person, is to be so passionate that your audience or client cannot help but acknowledge that you are both an expert and a confidant. When they see that, they begin to see the possibilities that your message and service offers. This is a long way from a feature-benefit-close mentality. This is a journey to a different stage, that of abundance, responsibility, and growth.

Yvonne Green

is a change agent who has worked with national and international educational organizations to create and implement programs to improve school success. She is a contributing author to *Community Schools in Action: Lessons from a Decade of Practice*. Yvonne is an experienced keynote speaker, conference panelist, and workshop leader. She has also spoken internationally on her favorite topic, prayer. Yvonne currently runs a life coaching practice, Loving Life Daily, http://lovinglifedaily.com, through which she empowers people to change their lives through the decisions they make.

Yvonne can be reached at yvonneg2020@gmail.com.

Note to Self: Five Keys to Becoming a Highly Sought Out Speaker

Yvonne Green

Y ou have to meet my wife," he said. "She has been looking to hire someone like you!" I was taken off guard, surprised, and happy...very happy.

I had volunteered to do a free workshop for parents at the local Parent Teachers Association (PTA). My only expectation was to have a good time and get invited back. But, I got a $25 honorarium from the PTA as well as a strong recommendation from a parent that led to my first big consulting contract. Then, as a result of the first contract, I got a second long-term contract with another organization.

This is a very fond memory for me. It energizes me and gives me a sense of the abundant opportunities and possibilities awaiting me as a speaker. As I embark on a new chapter of my vision of being a highly sought out speaker, I have been revisiting this and other empowering memories. I come to these memories to find important lessons I can use to propel me into the reality of my vision.

It is said that our successes always leave us clues. So I am revisiting my success to look for some of the habits, values, practices, and attitudes that contributed to my accomplishments as a speaker. And in that process, I am creating notes to remind me what I need to focus on. Here are five of those notes to self:

Note to Self #1: Have a vision—it creates open doors. Early in my career as a social worker, I created a vision to be a highly sought out speaker on issues of emotional well-being for children and families. I got a lot of energy and joy from this vision, and although I was an unknown, I began to create my own opportunities to speak. I made presentations at staff meetings, at professional development events, and at conferences. I became a consultant, began offering workshops, and became a highly sought out speaker for one of my workshops.

To realize my vision, I searched for and took jobs that included speaking responsibilities. Before long, I was speaking at conferences at Harvard, Stanford, and Johns Hopkins. Having that vision helped me to "see" possibilities for myself, and made me bold enough to step into opportunities that came my way.

Today, I feel rusty and out of shape as a speaker, because I have been in transition for the last three years. I have relocated to a new state and have no current "following", and I have not yet spoken anywhere or on topics related to my vision. I feel somewhat intimidated by it all. And, I am still committed to being a highly sought out speaker. My new focus is to empower people to live their God-given purpose.

When I connect to this vision, I feel exhilarated and alive. This feeling makes me remember how exquisitely my previous vision played itself out and gave me opportunities beyond my wildest dreams. I know it will happen to me again because I have a vision, and vision creates open doors.

Note to Self #2: Love the topics I speak on. When I am passionate, curious, and deeply invested in the topics I speak on, I am thorough in my research. I develop a level of expertise in the topic that allows me to feel more confident, relaxed and fun. As a result, I deliver high quality content, respond more spontaneously to questions, and create rich, meaningful exchanges with the audience where we feel connected to each other. I've noticed that when I create these experiences for my audience, I get more business.

It was in this type of atmosphere that the parent told me his wife was looking to hire someone like me. And it was in a similar setting that an attendee referred me to my next big client.

As I resume speaking in this next phase of my life, I don't expect to speak only on topics I enjoy, but I hope to speak on those topics most of the time. The more invested I am in a topic, the greater the windfall for both my audience and me. So, how do I make this happen?

Simon Sinek, author of *Start with Why*, says that our goal should not be to work with everyone but with those who share our values. So I've decided that my goal is to speak primarily on topics that resonate with my values. If they connect with my values and vision, then the passion will come.

Note to Self #3: Open my own doors. Early in my speaking career, I asked friends to invite me to speak to their groups. I volunteered to be the keynote speaker at graduations. I provided free workshops at local libraries, in churches, and to youth-serving groups like Boys and Girls Clubs. I actively created opportunities for myself.

I recall meeting an Eskimo woman at a conference. We hit it off, and I told her I'd love to come to her village in Alaska to speak. A year later, I was speaking there and experiencing the life of a contemporary Eskimo. (I discovered that there are no igloos there!)

Moving forward, I must remember to let people know I would love the honor of speaking to their groups, organizations, or communities. When I ask, I am opening my own doors. When I don't ask, I am letting others take those opportunities. So, I will ask!

Note to Self #4: Add value. I believe that people come to hear me speak to get answers to challenges, increase their knowledge on a topic, connect with relevant resources, learn new strategies, and acquire skills to solve a problem or attain a goal. When I have focused on these in my presentations, I have added great value.

Years ago a client asked me to develop a workshop on helping children cope with the violence around them. She said I would speak to two groups of 30 people. The day of the conference, she said the workshop was oversubscribed and moved me to the main conference room. I had over 150 people in the room! Later that same day, I repeated the workshop to an audience of the same size. I did not expect such an overwhelming response to my workshop. I was really shocked. However, I understood I added high value to them by giving them insights and answers to a problem that kept them up at night. After the conference I was flooded with invitations to speak on this topic and became a highly sought out speaker!

Nancy Matthews, Co-Founder of Women's Prosperity Network, speaks of *The One Philosophy,* which says that wherever we are, we can be the answer for at least one person. My goal as a speaker is to be The One for my audience. When people come to hear me speak, they are looking to solve a problem or meet a goal. I am not so naïve to think I will have all the answers and be all things to all people. However, if I take the time to understand my audience's needs and aspirations, and set my intentions to help them make some progress in those areas, I will always find a way to add value.

Note to Self #5: Manage feedback objectively. Event attendees usually have the opportunity to evaluate a speaker on how engaging, relevant, and responsive she was to the audience. In my first workshop evaluation, most attendees said I did an excellent job, but a few said I was not so good. Instead of assessing my performance based on the overwhelming positive responses, I obsessed over the few that said I was not good, and I beat up myself about it.

To prevent this from happening again, I decided to take a more objective approach going forward and let the numbers do the talking. I decided to look at the total responses and not focus on isolated responses. Another thing I have done and will continue to do is to ask my host to share the tool that will be used to get feedback from attendees. Knowing what I will be evaluated against helps me give attention to those things in my speech.

So, to fulfill my vision to be a highly sought out speaker, I need to remember my five notes to self: (1) have a vision, (2) love the topics I speak on, (3) open my own doors, (4) add value, and (5) manage feedback objectively. These five reminders, when put into practice, will surely create a path for me to become a highly sought out speaker.

Carla Ureña Hutchinson

began studying dance in her hometown of St. Petersburg, Florida. She attended prestigious summer dance intensives including The Royal Winnipeg Ballet, Boston Ballet, and The Vaganova Festival. She studied at the North Carolina School of the Arts as a freshman in high school and by 15 began a pre-professional career as an apprentice of the Bay Ballet Theater in Tampa, and later Orlando's Southern Ballet Theater. After high school, Carla moved to Tallahassee, FL, and attended Florida State University where she earned a BS in Psychology, an MS, and a PhD in Instructional Systems Design. She has worked in both managerial and technical positions, with clients including the US Army and Navy. Now, as a wife and mother, she is delighted to combine her passion for learning and love of the arts to help maximize children's potential as the Director of *ARTS AfterSchool*.

For information about ARTS, visit www.TallyARTS.com.

My Journey from the Stage to Accidental Entrepreneur

Carla Ureña Hutchinson

When I was presented with the opportunity to contribute to a book alongside several of my friends and mentors, I jumped on board right away not fully acknowledging (or perhaps unconsciously overlooking) the topic of the publication was actually public speaking. You see, I have two "fears" in life: cockroaches and public speaking. How ironic it is, that I sit backstage in the green room of Ruby Diamond Auditorium at Florida State University with my 12-year-old ballet shoes squeezing my toes. Apparently dance shoes, even when well-worn do not care that your once slender body and strong, athletic feet have softened and spread with age and the birth of two children. The last time I was on this end of the FSU campus I was going to college starting out my career in the Psychology Department and performing with the Dance Department.

I am a first-generation American born into a Hispanic family who emigrated from Mexico before my brother and I were born. My father was a good provider allowing my mother to devote herself fully to rushing us around town. Between the two of us, we engaged in a plethora of enrichment activities including dance, soccer, water skiing, flute, piano, violin, dirt bike, tennis, and horseback riding. I quickly narrowed down my classes to those offered in the dance studio and by the age of 11 began attending summer dance intensives abroad, and at 14 moved to attend the North Carolina School of the Arts. My short-lived pre-professional career began at 15 and was abruptly ended with a back injury when I was 17 but I feel like I grew up on stage. Dancing is what helped me develop into the person I am today. The title of this book, *Journey to the Stage*, caught my eye, and I couldn't help but think how my story is more a journey *from* the stage. My entire early life and formative years, I felt at home on stage and performing for audiences small and large, that is, as long as I didn't have to open my mouth.

From College to Accidental Entrepreneur

After retiring my pointe shoes, I began my journey through undergraduate, master's, and doctoral degrees. I enjoyed school and the general coursework, as long as it didn't involve presentations. I quickly learned I was truly horrified by the thought of having to talk to groups even if I knew everyone in the "audience" and had a very good grasp on the content. In retrospect, I really don't know how I earned a PhD while working at a research institute managing military projects without facing my fear of public speaking.

After the birth of our second child, my mother approached me with a business idea. She wanted to start an arts program to assist children in developing self-esteem and other life skills. You see, my mother is a medical and therapeutic foster parent who, at the time of this writing, has cared for some 60 children over the course of 15 years. She saw firsthand, not only with her own children, but also with the many who lived in her home, how important regular engagement in extracurricular activities can be for children. She was given a sum of money as part of her inheritance from her parents, therefore we didn't need a formal business plan for financing purposes. One week later, with my father's encouragement and the support of my eternally loving and supportive husband, *ARTS AfterSchool* was born. I made a leap of faith and went from a very well-paid instructional systems designer working with military contracts to starting a brick and mortar business with no entrepreneurial experience and no income.

We quickly signed the lease on a store front and began the process of trying to turn a pie-shaped shell in the corner of a strip mall into a functional, welcoming space designed to house a program that would ignite creativity and fuel success for school aged children. In October of 2011, *ARTS AfterSchool* opened its doors, three months behind schedule and more than $60,000 over budget.

During the building process, I was advised to begin trying to market the program to help bring awareness to the program and help encourage enrollment. Lacking any business experience, I decided to join the Greater Tallahassee Chamber of Commerce. I attended the orientation/meet and greet and was asked to stand up and introduce myself. I felt a sudden rush of adrenaline and a familiar sinking feeling in the pit of my stomach. I had to open my mouth and talk to a small group of people. While I cannot actually recall what I said or how I said it, I clearly recall the feeling of dread. A kind lady approached me after the meeting and suggested I join a "leads group" to help build my marketing team. "You will get to know other people and have an opportunity to speak about your business, too," she said.

I was completely convinced I needed to attend these meetings and I also had to create a "30-second elevator speech." In retrospect, this seemingly simple task was the most overwhelming and fear-inducing experience. Somehow auditioning for dance companies, traveling out of the country alone to further my dance training, performing in front of audiences large and small, defending my dissertation, talking with military subject matter experts, and delivering military research reports at a distance was nothing compared to stringing a few sentences together to introduce myself and my business to a room full of people I may never see again.

Practice Makes Perfect

My time at FSU introduced me to some amazing researchers and to the large body of evidence on the topic of skill acquisition and expertise. The concept of 10,000 hours of deliberate practice being required to become an expert performer is a commonly accepted notion. I had no doubt that I could acquire the ability to speak, but I knew it would not be easy. My fellow Leads Group members witnessed and supported me through the painful, yearlong process of my reluctantly standing up to deliver my 30-second elevator speech every Wednesday. By year two, the anxiety had subsided and I no longer had butterflies in my stomach before it was my turn to speak. Nearly five years later, I am still not a fan of elevator speeches, but at least I don't have that adrenalin, fight or flight response anymore.

In an attempt to face my fear of speaking, I signed up for a Speaker's Boot Camp offered by Women's Prosperity Network where I had the pleasure to learn best practices for creating a compelling speech and techniques for delivering presentations. During the workshop I learned I am unapologetically passionate about bringing awareness to the importance of supporting our children so they acquire the necessary skills for lifelong success. It just makes so much sense that the single most important thing we can do for future generations is to invest in the success of our children today!

While I would love to end this story with socially acceptable measures of success, I cannot tell you that our business is "prospering" just yet. We have grown and are providing services to more families every day, but until now, neither my mother nor I have seen any financial benefit. We haven't taken a paycheck home or repaid the capital investment my mother made and my father ended up matching to help us grow, but I am pleased to say I feel truly happy. I have the best job in the world! I have been blessed to create the after school and summer programs for my two children and my niece and nephew to attend. Each and every day, I have the privilege of being surrounded by passionate teachers who love nothing more than to empower their students to grow and develop into happy, healthy, successful adults.

A few years ago, I used to look at my days on stage as the highlight of my life. Trading in my pointe shoes for a computer was not exactly easy. However, I now have a different perspective and believe my true, meaningful life began the moment I stepped off the stage and into the role of a wife, a mother, and a business owner. I am truly grateful for the friendships, skills, and overall life lessons I learned on my journey once I stepped off the stage and into this amazing life. I look forward to growing even more, learning to find my voice and building up the confidence to speak to groups in order to expand our ability to do even more for our community and local children. ARTS is growing and we are anxiously awaiting our move to a brand new, stand-alone building currently under construction. I am also excited about the non-profit, Foundation4ARTS, we recently created to better serve our community.

"Miracles are all around us just waiting for us to have the vision to see them." ~ Nancy Matthews

Melanie Berry,

Business and Life Coach, Public Speaker, Author, and Neuro Linguistic Programming (NLP) Practitioner, is a woman in her mid-50s with two amazing grown children, who loves her life and enjoys a variety of active hobbies including painting, travel and sailing. In 2001, she was diagnosed with a terminal illness after having suffered from symptoms for 20 years. Melanie was found to have more than 22 lesions throughout her body which doctors told her would eventually lead to complications that would cause her death. After fighting this, and other life-changing experiences, she gained a new understanding of her life's purpose. Melanie turned the lessons she learned into "My Recipes for Life - Keep Stirring the Pot," an engaging paradigm that teaches unconditional self-love, gratitude and trust. Melanie Berry is living proof that if you have recipes for life and keep stirring the pot, life can be Yummy.

You can contact Melanie at:
(973) 760-8039
info.myrecipesforlife@gmail.com
www.facebook.com/MelanieBerryMyRecipesForLife

My Recipes for Life ~ Keep Stirring the Pot

Melanie Berry

The game was called *Six Truths and a Lie,* a parlor game played at dinner parties with friends in Harlem.

1. I am an agent for change and speak on a multitude of subjects regarding My Recipes for Life - Keep Stirring the Pot.

2. I was adopted twice and found my birth father and 7+ siblings at age 55.

3. As a child, my household phones were tapped by the FBI because my father was involved in the Civil Rights Movement with Martin Luther King.

4. I was married three times and divorced once.

5. I was a member of a white-gloved, pearl-wearing, paramilitary group that raised huge amounts of money and taught me to stand up for myself.

6. I was diagnosed with a terminal illness that ate 12 holes in my brain and 10 holes in my spine. Presently, doctors cannot find any trace of those Swiss cheese holes in my body.

Which one is the lie?

Deepak Chopra says, "All of our fears in life can be traced back to the most fundamental one: not knowing who we are."

Facts Change - But Truths Are Unwavering and Universal

Melanie June Davis Berry Fraser Berry Simmons. I have had seven names in my life. Eight actually, as I still don't know what name my birth mother gave me.

Questions: "Melanie...What are you? Black, White, Latina?"

Those are the questions strangers, family, friends and I myself have had, all my life, about my ethnicity. Of course, like the good Unitarian Universalist that I was raised to be, I have generally had questions. However, in the past few years, I have discovered some answers, "Truths" as it were.

I Would Like to Share Some of Those Truths with You

Having seven names and identities, not knowing when or where I was born or by whom, I accumulated fears. Fear that I would be seen as the interloper that I was. Fear that I could not possibly belong, wherever I was, or anywhere, for that matter.

Being adopted not once but twice, I was plagued by a lingering feeling that in some way, I was unlovable. This feeling actually paralyzed me with fear and I dropped out of college for a year with agoraphobia. I could not leave the house.

Having your phones tapped by the FBI and watching the violence perpetrated against those in the Civil Rights Movement, including my mother, father and brother and other close family friends such as Martin Luther King and other scions of the Movement, made me sure that the world was a dangerous place. I felt unsafe and unprotected.

Was I married three times? True. I was married three times in three ceremonies to the same man. So, not feeling good enough and feeling trapped and alone at the end of my marriage was status quo. The divorce was horrific. It took its toll on all of us. The children and I ended up homeless and lived in a friend's attic for a time. Shame, defeat, and anger were just the tip of the iceberg of negative emotions and self-deprecating thoughts.

I became a highly successful part of wonderful corporate and volunteer organizations. One nonprofit was the Junior League, which my then husband called a white-glove, pearl-wearing paramilitary group. As usual, I was the only speck in the bowl of milk. Standing in the background, powerless and feeling alone, I integrated and diversified almost all my school, volunteer and work environments, blazing trails in my family's tradition. I pay my rent for the space that I take up here on earth, and for the air I breathe, by serving others. These activities are tiresome and lonely at best when you are wearing the team uniform but not really *on* the team. Being the "Only One" made me prone to always questioning my purpose.

After 42 misdiagnoses over a 20-year period, I was diagnosed with a terminal illness. The 42nd diagnosis, "It's all in your head," was given just days before doctors did the spinal tap and the 43rd and final diagnosis: Terminal. This could make one self-doubting and crazy. I felt both relieved and victimized by the diagnosis itself, more than by the disease.

So Since All Six of These Are True, What Is the Lie?

Today, I know I have all that I need to lead a happy, healthy and successful life. Today, I know I have the skill set to be a wonderfully successful speaker, standing in the lights, on a stage with microphone in hand and cameras rolling. I didn't always feel this way.

My body was hurting. I had no energy. Sitting still and quiet with my own thoughts was absolutely impossible. I needed constant monkey chatter and activities to help drown out my thoughts and depressed emotions. I certainly didn't believe or have faith in a higher power that was looking out for me. I was not listening to that still small voice inside me, my gut feeling or intuition.

I wanted a life partner, a soul mate. I didn't have one. I didn't believe I ever would have someone that would love, adore and protect me. My feelings of being unlovable were overwhelming.

There came a day when all of this weighed so heavily on me. I was in a speeding car, driving on the Florida Turnpike from the top of the state to the bottom. I spent the entire ride with my hand fearfully gripping the door handle. I didn't know whether to pull the door tightly closed or open it and fling myself into the traffic. I was really finished with my life.

What Changed?

It was my daughter who pulled it all together. She said, "Mommy, please...you have everything that you need. This is a chemical imbalance. The disease makes you depressed. The medications for the disease make you depressed. Having a terminal illness this debilitating causing you to take 26 meds a day would make anyone depressed. You have people that love and adore you. Life is wonderful! Please, Mommy, choose life. We need you!"

It was my daughter's pleading for me to live that was the catalyst for me to decide that I wanted to live and to be willing to change myself from the inside out.

I was hungry for a new way of experiencing life. I changed my mind and then I had to change the recipes for my life.

I began to change my habits with a definiteness of purpose. Initially, I had to stop and take a look at those habits. I had to look at my thinking and the radio station that I played in my head. Everything we have ever created in our life begins in our thoughts. Fear of change can be limiting until the pain of holding on is greater than the fear of letting go of debilitating and limiting beliefs. I began to ease up on my resistance to change and become willing to make changes. Moms Mabley said, "If you always do what you've always done, you'll always get what you've always got."

I applied faith. Through the study of teachings of great spiritual and metaphysical teachers sent to guide us out of the darkness of our illusions, I got in touch with new positive thoughts and people. I rid myself of all toxic people in my life, including family members. With a total of three families, that was a lot of possible toxicity for a woman who still doesn't know where she was born.

Someone once asked me how long I would spend with a smoker in a phone booth. I would NOT be in a phone booth with a smoker, at all, ever. That metaphor became my gauge for toxicity in people, places and thoughts.

I wrote everything down, very specifically, and visualized my new wonderful life with all the feelings, smells and thoughts that were to come with it. Playing the video of my future life as a part of my new self-discipline of a Positive Mental Attitude and accurate thinking in my daily routine. Creating mantras for literally each step I took on my daily walk.

In his book, *Master Key to Riches*, Napoleon Hill says, "Every mind needs friendly contact with other minds, for food of expansion and growth." A mastermind alliance. I found some like-minded, positive people. I joined a mastermind group, where each of the four of us had a terminal illness. We supported one another by meeting weekly, sharing our visions of a healthy, prosperous, abundant future. We devised a plan. We rewarded ourselves when we followed through. We shared our successes. This loving, supportive community nurtured us into wholeness, health and prosperity. I am happy to report that we have all recovered.

To get to feeling glorious, with dynamic energy, active and alive, you have to become clear on what you desire in and for your life. Be specific. Make sure to put wings on your prayers and desires to reach your goals. One of my goals was to speak publicly, regularly and profitably.

Commitment to myself and honoring those goals and visions with action steps allowed me to make meaningful changes in my mind, body and spirit. When I became honest with myself, I was crystal clear that being a paid speaker, on the stage with cameras rolling, was always where I visualized myself.

Weekly progress and accountability, in a loving supportive spiritual and business community where I am free to be myself, know myself, in a spirit of win-win-win instead of competition, has allowed me to take this fearless journey of self-discovery, health and success. I am now willing to recognize and acknowledge the magnificence that is ME.

The Lie?

The Lies were all those "Facts" that I kept seeing as my truth.

My Truth?

All of these "Truths" have conspired to make me who I am. I am a Spiritual Being having a physical experience. I deserve the best and I accept the best now.

My Recipe for Life

1 cup determination
1 cup courage
2 cups self-awareness
A dash of hope
Bake in your heart.
Sprinkle with faith.
Store in your soul.
Keep stirring the pot.

Cynthia Chevrestt,

single mom, teacher and military leader, now speaker, author and Professional Life Coach, provides coaching and programs for women to overcome the challenges and burdens that accompany their vast responsibilities. Her passion for coaching single mothers and female veterans comes from her own struggles and challenges of being a single mom, especially while serving in support of Operation Iraqi Freedom for 18 months during 2003-2004. Wrought with her own struggles with depression, guilt and stress (just to name a few,) Cynthia sought a solution for herself through extensive research and education. The result was a complete transformation of her own life and the creation of The Winning Formula to a Great Life: a complete life shift from just getting by and surviving to thriving and thoroughly enjoying the awesome responsibilities of being a mother, educator and military leader.

You can contact Cynthia at:
chevy@cynthiachevrestt.com
www.cynthiachevrestt.com

From Unworthy to Unstoppable

Cynthia Chevrestt

I could barely hear anything else in the room but my sporadic breathing and faint voices. I anxiously walked up to the front of the room. I didn't introduce myself nor did I say the title of my speech. I just read the first few sentences in an inaudible, quavering voice. Professor Rivera asked me to stop, take a deep breath, and start again but to speak up this time. I heard whispers and faint giggles. I saw their faces. They were embarrassed for me. I wanted to run out of the classroom, but that would have been even more humiliating. I knew I should have skipped the class like I normally would have whenever I was going to be put on the spot. I didn't mind taking a grade reduction. I was comfortable and content with sitting in the back of the room, lost in the crowd. I think Professor Rivera knew he made a mistake because he stopped me midsentence and asked me to take a seat while patting my shoulder. I missed two classes from my Puerto Rican studies class after that, hoping everyone would forget. Back to obscurity, my comfort zone.

That pretty much was my life. I loved joking, sharing stories, listening and talking to people. I truly loved people, especially children. But I didn't like standing out in front of a crowd. While growing up in the projects in Brooklyn, I didn't have many opportunities to stand out and be noticed. I wasn't involved in any sports or any other extracurricular activities.

As long as I showed up in school, did my homework and passed my tests, I was okay.   I was very shy, insecure and believed whatever I said wasn't important enough for anyone to want to hear. My small group of friends and family were enough. But I knew that if I was going to become a teacher one day, I had to learn to speak in front of a classroom. Early Childhood Education was my focus. I worked in a day care for eight years with the little ones. They were so sweet, innocent and nonjudgmental. They laughed with me, not at me. I felt safe.

After the Persian Gulf War in 1992, I decided to join the Army Reserves. Although it was a huge stretch for me, joining the service was one of my childhood dreams. I was 22 and had never been away from home. I was scared out of my mind, but it was what I needed. I wanted to see the world outside the projects. I needed the structure and discipline. I wanted to know that I was more than what I thought I was. I needed to face my fears. No one knew of my insecurities. It was a fresh start, a clean slate. My plan was to serve my country for eight years while I taught public school. I had a feeling the Army was going to change me forever.

I began my teaching career in an inner city elementary school out of Farragut projects in Brooklyn. It was a tough environment, but I felt right at home. Many of the students were challenging, but I understood them. They had tough exteriors, with experiences no child should have to endure. They were beautiful, smart, loving children that just needed a chance. They didn't trust easily but, when they did, their potential for academic and social brilliance blossomed and so did their grades. For some reason, my principal felt I was capable of conducting workshops along with other teachers on special education and other programs. As terrified as I was of speaking in front of my peers, the teachers were receptive and enjoyed the workshops, especially since they were delivered with humor. A few of the teachers and I would do skits, playing the parts of students and teachers creatively introducing new programs. My principal saw something in me that I didn't see in myself.

One morning during my third year of teaching, on September 11, 2001, my life as well as the lives of thousands of others changed forever. Through the windows of the second floor of our school building, we witnessed the Twin Towers and their destruction. I remember the screams and cries as if it were yesterday. There was complete pandemonium. Parents hysterically rushed into classrooms snatching their frightened children, rushing out in fear of another terrorist attack. Shortly after that, I realized I was also living in fear. I waited for the year to end before I put my furniture in storage, donated some stuff, including my broken down car, and told my kids to pack whatever toys fit in their backpacks and we were off. I left their mentally abusive father behind to start a new life in Florida.

After several months spent establishing new beginnings, I was deployed for 18 months in support of Operation Iraqi Freedom. I spent a few months traveling from state to state before I was sent to Kuwait for the remaining 8 months. I left my children with my sister for a couple of months and eventually flew them back to New York to live with their father for a year. I prayed he would treat them better than he treated me. I had to explain to anyone caring for my children the plan if anything were to happen to me.

It's been over 12 years, and I still get very emotional about that time in my life as I type this. Completing my mission as a soldier was the easy part; leaving my children was the most difficult of all. While I was overseas, my ex did not allow me to speak to my children for months. Upon my return, as people thanked me and my school welcomed me with open arms with a ceremony in my honor, again I felt this feeling of unworthiness. During my deployment, I was promoted, given awards including a Meritorious Service medal and won Non Commissioned Officer of the Year. None of that mattered to me.

One day, while watching my son's basketball game, one of the mothers asked me where I had been. I told her I had been deployed. As a few of the moms that overheard thanked me for my service, one mom declared in disbelief that she couldn't believe I left my children. I remember her clearly saying that if it were her, they would have to send her to jail or kill her before she left her children. Although the other mothers argued that I had no choice, the disbelieving mom only confirmed what I was feeling all along. I had failed as a mother.

For years I tried to make up for lost time. I became the overindulgent mother, never saying no to her children. I was their mother, father and friend. I taught, tutored, worked the afterschool program and continued in the Army Reserves to support that lifestyle and a house I couldn't afford with no child support. I became tired, overwhelmed, stressed, angry, broke and depressed. I felt I had no right to complain or share my burden. I had been away long enough that I shouldn't be so selfish. I was running on empty. It wasn't until a therapist told me I was depressed and recommended that I take medication that I decided to change my life and finally work on myself. I didn't want medication, but I did want to be a good mom with happy and healthy children. I was on a new mission. This time it was a mission to fill up my own tank. To give to myself what I needed in order to be the best mom and woman I could be. I read books, biographies, and articles; watched videos; and listened to audio CDs (among other things) about healthy, wealthy, happy, successful people. I wanted to know what they did that I needed to do. I invested in my education and self-development. I did whatever I could afford to do to make myself a better person and a better mom. I was beginning to feel worthy.

It's been over ten years now and I can honestly say I've accomplished that mission. I took 100% responsibility for my life and developed effective daily habits that fulfilled me and my purpose each day. Since then, I have resigned from teaching, sold my home, and simplified my life. My children and I are happy and living wonderful lives. I still come across challenges but I now have the tools that get me by without the guilt.

After 23 years in the service, I am a First Sergeant of a drill sergeant company in Ft. Lauderdale. I've had many opportunities to speak to soldiers and leaders. I have created programs to raise morale with my company and battalion. Although I resigned as a public school teacher, I am still a teacher. I just teach on a different platform. My new mission is to empower and inspire women, especially single moms and female veterans, to live their best lives. I love coaching women, giving workshops and seminars, and speaking to groups on stage. I still get nervous, but once I begin to deliver my message and serve my purpose, I'm unstoppable. As I look back on my life, I realize that all the obstacles and adversities were meant to teach me something and, in turn, teach others. My principal back in New York saw something in me that I now see in myself. I am worthy, and I have a responsibility to share my brilliance.

What advice would I give to someone considering their own Journey to the Stage?

Be authentic and stay true to yourself and your message. You will never please everyone so you might as well start with pleasing yourself.

Have a sense of humor. Sometimes things don't always go the way you plan. Don't sweat the small stuff and enjoy the journey. People will love you for it.

You are responsible for your message. No one else can deliver it the way you can.

"Breaking News: You are always in the right place at the right time. The difference maker ... the right attitude, choices and actions." ~ Susan Wiener

Martin D. Butler

was born in St. Andrews, Scotland. He has five sisters and is the proud father of two sons, Glenn and Dean. He first came to the United States in 2000, quickly advanced to Special Projects and Regional Operations Manager and is regarded as one of the top minds in the industry. He attributes all his success in business today to his desire to learn, and he models his principles based on those of Thomas Edison, Andrew Carnegie, and Henry Ford. His new book, *The IOU Book*, is scheduled for release in the fall of 2015. He makes his home today in Fort Myers, Florida.

Contact information:
cell (239) 313-1141 (text only)
office (239) 400-0123 (open 24/7)
ioubook@martindbutler.com (private)

Finding the Voice Within

Martin Butler

Having travelled around the world and extensively through the USA as a Senior Project Manager, specializing in heavy industry—oil rig construction, refineries, power plants and numerous nuclear facilities—I find myself in very unfamiliar territory. By all accounts, I shouldn't even want to write this chapter or stand in front of people and speak. I have dyslexia – writing is pure Hell for me. My Scottish accent is so thick it even shows up in my typing. To add insult to injury, I'm also a shy and introverted guy.

Until I came to America, I never even realized I was bilingual. So to help you understand me a little bit better, please *STOP* reading *right now* and on that smart phone that you never let out of your sight, visit

www.YouTube.com: Burnistoun -
Voice Recognition Elevator in Scotland.

I promise that you will love this 3-minute sketch. It's hilarious, enjoy!

Number 11 - brilliance!

Anyway, despite the numerous challenges I have faced both personally and professionally, why, oh, why would I take such drastic action and suddenly decide to become a bestselling author and recognized international speaker? I'm not here to bait you with stories, because we all have "ah-ha" moments, we all have tragedies; we all have moments of clarity that are tremendous waypoints in our own journey. I have been there, and done that, and now I actually think I have more t-shirts than my good friend, Varsha Bhongade, despite her being in the clothing business. However, on the week of 08/11/11, nothing could have prepared me for the most defining moments of my entire life. Moments so profound it has taken me over 3 years and countless miles of travel and hours of study to make a simple decision and go public with my findings in the form of my first universal bestseller seen at www.theioubook.com.

The full title, and the message contained within the same, is actually a simple yet very powerful and highly encrypted equation on the same standing as $E=mc^2$. An Enigma code so to speak; it's pure genius! When it is produced and marketed effectively, it can and will send a shock wave around the world creating a huge shift in people's mindset. The title alone can be turned into 3 separate volumes.

Now flash forward to the present day. As the speaker on the stage, whether you are training a group or recommending a product, you are the "Leader" and "Trusted Authority". All eyes are on you, and the entire audience knows that you are the expert. Without you, they would not have come. They would not take off from work, drive or fly across towns and states, and leave families and businesses behind. They are there to see *you* and *you, my friend have to show up as your best self and deliver that message and be of service. You become "The One"!*

However, on a lighter note, becoming *"The One"* is a simple and easy process and your stage doesn't have to be a physical stage with an audience of 360 people like I had in Los Angeles on my very first speaking engagement. We all have to grow and growth is a choice so you can simply "expand" your comfort zone. Not "get out of it," expand it! To be honest, I left the world of heavy engineering and what many Americans would see as an amazing six-figure salaried job at the top of my profession, because of that need to *expand*.

However, working in that environment - especially in the nuclear industry - you become very anal in your approach and that can be a pain in the ass, trust me. Take that trusty smart phone we used a moment ago and Google "images for Scottish Bar Stools"...

Now, a lot of people would think that the smarter move may have been to hang my shingle as a consultant, jack up my fees, and be a contractor. That would have easily gotten me more money, but it was never just about money. You know that. I had the need to grow and to help others, to embrace the idea of a servant's mentality. Besides, with a name like Butler, what chance do I have?

So at the top of my profession, I left. A little spontaneous, I know, but I needed to do it. I immersed myself in the world of real estate. I sought out experts in the Live Out Loud community, the Secret Knock, Women's Prosperity Network and coaches and cohorts such as Randy Tate and Loral Langemeier. I flew all over the world to take part in seminars such as 3 Days to Cash, the Big Table, and The Prosperity UN-Conference, to name but a few. In all of them, I found a level of clarity and passion, and, shall I say – intimacy - among those people and groups that the W2 world could never approach. I also saw the power of what happens when we all start working together with a common view of the world. These people spoke about "true honest values" which aligned perfectly with my own HEARTFELT PASSIONS. Again, because

I am a Scotsman, the passion that runs through my veins on so many levels is off the charts. It actually can scare a lot of people.

Stepping into that YES! ENERGY is amazing, having VISION BEYOND SEEING is awesome and stepping into your DESTINY with complete conviction and commitment...now that's LIVING! This is the place where MAGIC starts to happen! You find yourself doing things you never thought possible or could ever have imagined since you were a child. You find FREEDOM!!!

The first time I attended Loral Langemeier's *3 Days to Cash*, all my senses were on fire. The very first day, I knew I had to keep up that expansion and sign up for her Big Table coaching in Lake Tahoe, and I was the first in the room to do so along with my first son, Glenn. Then I realized that the Tahoe coaching would not be for another five months! That was absolutely not going to work for me. On the other hand, I could attend the next Big Table in Australia in 9 days... of course, that was the other side of the world. No problem! Of course, I was up for the journey, but how I managed to get there for the event totally defies logic and common sense. Technically I should never have been issued a visa given the five days of processing required. I applied for the visa on Monday night and was issued my entry visa on Wednesday evening. I booked the flight and accommodation right then, and on Thursday I was in the air heading to Sydney, Australia.

I later found out that I was the first person to make such a journey within the whole Live Out Loud community. Loral both acknowledged and rewarded me by assigning me to her Master Coach and business partner, Randy Tate. My ultimate goal, as I later told him, was simple. It was not money; it wasn't the fancy car in the driveway. I simply wanted to FIND MY VOICE.

Seven months later I'm heading to Los Angeles to speak at a seminar in front of 360 people, a marketing boot camp, really, but not as the keynote. In fact, I had the stage for a whopping five minutes. More than one of my mentors thought I was crazy. Loral Langemeier, who probably thought I had been out in the sun too long, called and gave me one of the best pep talks I ever received, and I was as ready as I ever would be.

At that time, I was discussing a financial product that, due to SEC regulations and the company's own rules, I actually could not mention by name. Challenged? Yes. I accepted that by branding myself. I was no longer an affiliate of the company, I *was* the company. Let me tell you, there is something really special when you brand yourself, a huge mindset shift takes place. I could control the audience by turning up as my true authentic self ... with Loral's words ringing in my ear, "Martin you need to nail it; you need to nail it."

So there I stood, in front of a crowd of 360 strangers who had *not* come to see me talk about a product that I *couldn't* refer to by name, and I had five whole minutes. After Craig Duswalt introduced me, I only had four-and-a-half minutes left! With the clock ticking, my mind just blanked out. Talk about pressure! I held firm, refocused, rambled a bit, and then got back on track. With very little interaction from the audience, I was sure I blew it.

I had hoped I would get 10 people. I would have been astonished with 50. When the break came and the audience could move, there was literally a stampede in my direction, I got 131 inquiries. Now, in the interest of full disclosure, there were some duplicates. The actual number I ended up with was 106. I couldn't have cared less. Yes! Yes!! Yes!!! I had NAILED IT.

"The seeds you plant today are the foundation of what will grow tomorrow. Today plant seeds of love, kindness, faith and belief in yourself and your dreams." ~ Nancy Matthews

Kathy Pendleton

has more than 25 years experience as a technical trainer with various computer software companies. Kathy has spent a few years transitioning into the arena of personal development and inspirational messages. Her pursuit of excellence in communications is continuing in her current activities. Her special gifts are in creating simple step-by-step explanations to make complex subjects understandable. While still fascinated by the intricacies of computer software, her passion is now focused on personal growth, daily disciplines, and interpersonal connections. She is developing her skills in public speaking to increase her reach in these areas. The driving force behind it all is the creation of "light bulb moments" for herself and others. Kathy lives in San Jose, California, with her husband Tom. She's the founder of her business, Messages of Prosperity, which emails messages of inspiration and motivation as her gift to her subscribers.

Contact Kathy through www.MessagesOfProsperity.com.

Plan, Take Action, Evaluate, Revise, Repeat

Kathy Pendleton

I bet that, if I met you, I could learn what you love and get you talking about it. I would ask a few questions, notice the animation when you answer, and pretty quickly you'd be engaged and filling me in on what you know well or what you feel strongly about. During my first job, I was asked to go on an interview dinner, because my colleagues couldn't manage to get our prospect talking. During the evening, I was successful! Wouldn't it be wonderful if speaking to a group were as comfortable as speaking with an individual?

"90% of how well the talk will go is determined before the speaker steps on the platform." ~ Somers White

Preparation Is Key

When I was a senior in high school, I ran for class treasurer. During the campaign I was very excited about having prepared the perfect speech. Unfortunately anticipation and execution did not coincide. Have you ever started to speak before an audience and felt them pulling away from you? In front of 634 classmates, I experienced the sad realization that I was crashing and burning. Afterwards my best friend said that if I'd practiced with her she would've told me how terrible the speech was. I was totally humiliated, lost the election and had to attend school every day weighed down by embarrassment. Thank goodness nobody but me remembers it.

Speech class in college was a triumph! I loved it and excelled. The structure reeled me in from the free-form ramble that had contributed to my earlier downfall. I still believed in what I was saying, but I was learning a way to organize my thoughts into a succinct and impactful delivery. Speaking in front of a group produced anxiety, but not enough to keep me from obtaining a minor in secondary education. Then I avoided the question entirely by accepting a job in computer software development. After only a few years, I experienced the lure of technical training.

"We learn by practice." ~ *Martha Graham*

Practice and Find Your Niche

The move into the technical education department felt like going home. Whoever said that the best way to learn a subject is to teach it wasn't kidding! The challenge and intrigue were in creating explanations that students understood, determining the order of presentation of various topics, and recognizing the difference between language that clarified and language that confused. It was wonderful! I felt alive and fulfilled.

The classroom experience was exciting to me. I loved figuring out how to explain a complex concept, restating and revising to find a better way, and discovering questions that would reveal exactly what detail was unclear. I also valued having a week or two to cover a subject, because it provided the time flexibility if it was needed. Working with colleagues to devise a better presentation sequence, so that just as the students were about to ask a question, the answer appeared in the lecture and created one of those "light bulb" moments—that really put a grin on my face!

"Believe in yourself, take on your challenges, dig deep within yourself to conquer fears. ~ Chantal Sutherland

A Curve Ball

My company began to expand internationally and I was selected to deliver many of the international classes. As a high school foreign exchange student, I had previously experienced the challenge of language and cultural differences. The expansion of relationships, understanding, and acceptance was worth the discomfort of these situations. It required constant focus and awareness, and it broadened my perspective. I had never been particularly tactful before, but it was necessary to be observant and flexible to effectively serve the students. Did you know that there are English words that are just fine to use in the U.S., but not in the U.K., and vice versa? I learned that once or twice the hard way.

"If you don't like something, change it. If you can't change it, change your attitude." ~ Maya Angelou

Restructuring

After many years in the training department, filled with enriching experiences, I left the corporate training world. Today I'm beginning to speak in front of groups. To my surprise, I've learned that technical training and public speaking are quite different. I was terrified! That old senior class speech came back out of the dark ages to haunt me. I had no idea that its impact was so strong that it would inhibit my willingness to write and to speak in public.

I needed a coach to move past this mental block and develop new skills. I learned that the goal in public speaking is establishing an emotional connection with the audience. I was not in the habit of opening up and feeling vulnerable in front of a room of strangers, and the exercises to delve deeper into my emotions and create vulnerability were difficult and exhausting. I had developed friendships with students, but there was no emotion in the content of my training message.

Coaching has provided insights into flaws with both my message and my delivery—flaws that lead to a poor response from my audience. I'm working to tighten up my rambling style. The details, which are so important to me, create confusion and boredom in others—so I just eliminate them. My goal is to craft a message that produces impact and empathy. I want to present only the essential points of a story to create focus and clarity for the listener and to make it easy to distill a lesson worth discussing.

"Understand to achieve anything requires faith and belief in yourself, vision, hard work, determination, and dedication."
~ Gail Devers

Integration

The journey is far from over for me. All the challenges, failures, humiliations and successes have contributed to the person, presenter and speaker I've become. Tactfulness still requires my attention to have empathy for the other person. Impact and brevity create the opportunity to practice my editing skills. The vulnerability to create connection continues to be a work in process. But when the audience connection is made, the point of all the study is clear. The "light bulb" goes on in the eyes and hearts of the listeners, lights up my soul and the feeling is magical—magical enough to keep me dedicated to moving forward in this new career.

Johnny Regan

is an internationally recognized speaker, educator, consultant, executive coach, seminar leader and author of the upcoming book, *Live Your Vision Change the World.* Johnny is known to his clients as "The Vision Maker." Les Brown calls him "Mr. Charisma!"

Johnny can be reached at www.JohnnyRegan.com.

The Joy of Speaking

Johnny Regan

Speaking is one of the oldest and most respected art forms on the planet—and the most powerful. I know of no greater joy than walking off a stage to thunderous applause knowing you have connected and made a difference in the lives of others.

To speak is to put things in motion, to love and to affirm, to dance into the hearts of those who hear your message, to let them know that their life is worth living at the highest level possible, that everything is a possibility to those who believe in their vision. You speak, and behold... lives are changed.

Here are some tips that have helped me to experience The Joy of Speaking:

> *"And I will know my song well before I start singing."*
> *~ Bob Dylan*

1. Know Your Topic

First and foremost, you need to know what you are talking about. If people are giving you their time, you must deliver and give them the goods.

The first speech I gave was in Mr. Peterson's seventh grade history class. My subject was Thomas Edison. I mastered my topic. I ferociously read everything I could on the great inventor. I even visited his home and took the full guided tour twice. When it was my turn to speak, I had a little piece of paper with three words of reminders on it. I extemporaneously delivered my speech. I had all my classmates' attention. I delivered. When I was done, Mr. Peterson said, "Excellent!!" And he asked me to show my classmates my notes. Everyone was amazed that I only had three words. They applauded. I had inspired them. Before my speech, most kids just read their speeches from index cards. From then on, most just used notes. That day was the first day I experienced The Joy of Speaking because I knew my topic.

"The most original writers borrowed one from another."
~ Voltaire

2.   Study the Speakers That You Love

The best way to find your own voice is to first sing in the key of the speakers you want to be like. Study them. Two of my favorite speakers growing up were Billy Graham and Les Brown. When I was 22, I took a two-day bus ride to see Billy Graham speak. When I got to the auditorium, the first 100 rows of seats were taken. So I walked up to the front row center aisle and sat down on the floor. I was maybe 15 feet from the podium! I prayed. When the security lady came to tell me I couldn't sit there on the floor, I began to plead and tell her how I just took a 48-hour bus ride to see Reverend Graham.

She replied, "I'm sorry, sir, but you cannot sit here!"

Just then someone began to introduce Billy Graham and the applause began. I rose to my feet and, with all my exuberance, I waved and welcomed him. I kept praying. Now I don't know if angels hauled the security lady off, but when I sat back down, she was gone. No security!

Billy Graham was now standing on stage right in front of me. I remember him being tall, strong, handsome and confident. Powerful but gentle. Great presence. Charisma. What I remember most was that he spoke with authority.

When I speak on the topic of vision, I speak with the authority I learned from Billy Graham.

Les Brown has always been my favorite motivational speaker. I love his enthusiasm, his quotes, his energy, his humor and his storytelling! I consume his books and tapes.

In 2002 I was asked to be the Master of Ceremonies for a two-day success expo at the Miami Hyatt, and Les Brown was going to be the keynote trainer and speaker. I was going to work with and introduce my hero!

When the weekend arrived, I was a great emcee because I was having a blast. I gave Les one of the greatest introductions of my lifetime. He blew the roof off the house!!!

Later that night I was in the gift shop, and I heard Les's voice: "Johnny, you did amazing this weekend! You have a gift." He said that people pay him thousands of dollars to learn to speak, but he could not teach them what I have, a unique gift for speaking! That changed the course of my thoughts on speaking. He taught me to realize what a privilege it is to speak, that speaking is an art form that must be honed and crafted.

"It's all about the fans..." ~ *Bruce Springsteen*

3. It's Not About You

I cannot express the importance of knowing that "It is not about you" when taking the stage to speak. It is about delivering for them, your audience. You are there to be a contribution; to inspire, to educate, to move people to the higher angels of their nature. If you remember this, you can lose most of your fears of speaking.

In April of 2013, I had breakfast with Nancy Matthews, Founder of Women's Prosperity Network. Nancy is known as "The Visionary with Guts" and I am known as "The Vision Maker." Nancy thought it would be great if we teamed up and did something called The Vision Tour together. I thought it was a brilliant idea and about a month later we were on our first leg of the tour in Melbourne, Florida.

Nancy started the morning off with a bang, and for about an hour the audience hung on her every word. Then she introduced me and brought me up. I started my talk off by pointing out and praising someone in the audience who was brave and vulnerable. I recognized her courage and said, "I will try to show the same courage all day." Nancy and I rocked and it was one of my all-time favorite days of speaking.

When we got back in the car to go home, Nancy turned to me and high-fived me. She said, "Johnny, you are the real deal!"

"What do you mean?" I asked.

She said, "I have never seen you speak before and it is always a risk touring with someone. Some speakers make it about themselves, but you made it about them!"

Nancy and I continued the tour and impacted countless lives and made great money, too! As of this writing, Nancy Matthews is one of my dearest friends in the whole world.

If you realize your speaking is about others, you will fully experience the joy of speaking.

"Nothing great was ever achieved without enthusiasm"
~ *Ralph Waldo Emerson*

4. True Enthusiasm Can Carry You Far

Once I was booked to be the keynote speaker at a high school anti-drug rally. I was to speak to 11th and12th graders. I prepared my speech accordingly and mastered my topic. To my horror, when I arrived, I saw a gymnasium full of student ages 5-17! How could I possibly speak on anti-drugs for an hour to kids from kindergarten to twelfth grade, especially after they had already heard from five other speakers on the topic!?!

I made a call to my friend, Mike, who has been a youth pastor for over 30 years to ask for help. He said, "What? You can't speak to a group of those ages together. They are living in different worlds. Are these people crazy? You can't do it."

He was of little help. But he did say he would pray for me, and I did need all the prayers I could get. As I sat there listening to the other speakers talking about how bad drugs are, I could see the kids dozing off. And it was still an hour until I was going to speak! I prayed. There was no way I could go with my prepared speech.

Ten minutes before I was to speak, Mike called me back and said, "Johnny, you have natural gifts. Kids love you. Go inside and ask God to guide you.

I prayed for God to make it about them and give me true enthusiasm. God answered. I started speaking about what a vision is and told them how cool they all were and that they couldn't live their vision and do drugs. They all agreed. Then I began to ask them what their visions where. The floodgates burst open. Kids of every age went wild!

"*My name is Jeremy and my vision is to be a forensic scientist.*"
"*My name is Dorothy and my vision is to be a veterinarian!*"
"*My name is Alex and my vision is to be a football player!*"
"*My name is Dana and my vision is to be a singer!*"
"*My name is Kerry and my vision is to be a teacher!*"

I prayed for God to make it about them and give me enthusiasm. God delivered. True enthusiasm never fails!

May we all fully experience The Joy of Speaking as we continue our Journey to the Stage!

"We may not have it all together, but together we have it all."
~ Anonymous

Sandra Hanesworth

is the founder of the A-List Connection, a unique company that unites individuals with passionate experts in health, career, travel, and love. She has developed a system for helping people to focus on building, nurturing, and maintaining lifelong relationships while achieving business goals. Sandra is thrilled to be the Northern California Chapter Leader for Women's Prosperity Network, and supports the WPN community as a coach, strategist and yes, speaker, too. While Sandra loves jumping on planes to work with individuals and communities all over the world, she calls the San Francisco Bay Area home and knows her greatest blessings are her three children, Justin, Sarah, and Victoria.

You can contact Sandra at:
(510) 557-8849
Sandra@AListConnection.com
www.AListConnection.com

The Accidental Speaker

Sandra Hanesworth

More than once in my speaking career, I have been asked, "Sandra, what makes a good speaker?" After all, I have spent years as a speaker, coach, and strategist; I should be able to rattle off a laundry list of traits that good speakers share. I'm known for helping people to break through the barriers they have built. In the end, though, speaking is just the glass that holds a great wine. The beauty and enjoyment of that wine is dependent on the knowledge of the person who has poured it and the desire of the person who holds the glass. I speak to serve, and I aspire to help others in their quest to speak their passions, from the heart. That is what makes a good speaker.

It has only taken a lifetime to learn that.

Even as a child, I was fascinated with how humans behave. I remember watching talk shows as a child and trying to see the influence of body language on how people really communicated. I could not have told you, at the time, that was what I was doing, but years later, I can see it. I was fascinated with the idea of how people could get up in front of an audience and speak, on *any* subject ... especially since I was so scared of it.

Did I say scared? Abject terror would be a better term. As a student, I was frozen with fear by the idea of getting up in front of others and speaking. I was the kid that stuttered. Hilarity was sure to ensue. Surprisingly, I made it through school without dying of fear due to an impending book report given in front of the class, and, as a young businesswoman, my father gave me the advice to join Toastmasters. Now, I don't know which version of Toastmasters that Dad had gone to, but his description and my reality were polar opposites. I left in a panic attack, sweat pouring off my body, and I quickly confirmed with myself that public speaking served no purpose.

Twenty-five years later, I move easily from one-on-one conversations to the stage and back again. What changed?

My philosophy. You see, sometimes we get all the answers we need, but we lack the support structure to believe we can achieve them. One of my first mentors was my Aunt Dolly, and she told me, long ago, to invest in knowledge and to always be prepared, because when opportunity knocks, you need to be able to give a confident "Yes!"

That driving philosophy in my life's work is to serve others through my business of helping people create shifts that enable them to set and achieve their objectives. Engaging in the journey to that goal made me realize that to ever *really* be able to meet and help others better themselves, I had to do the same thing. My Dad taught me that if it was worth doing it was worth doing at full throttle, so I redoubled my efforts and invested the time and effort to be the best in my business and take a servant's mentality in all things. My Mom had proved time and again that speaking from the heart was the only way to speak. Simple math told me that to reach more people, I had to speak to more people. The numbers don't lie, and in order to achieve my goals, I knew I had to face those fears of the stage. I went back and studied why certain speakers moved me. I realized that they took me to a place somewhere in myself that stimulated my desire for success and pushed me to reach my goals.

So, much to my chagrin, I embraced speaking the way you look forward to seeing the dentist when you know he's going to put in a filling. It's going to hurt, but the alternative is even worse. If I choose not to take the stage to teach, others lose. They continue to be unfulfilled in their lives. Yep. No pressure.

Was this easy? NO! In a speaker's workshop, I was reduced to that same child from grade school. Stuttering and stammering, I could barely talk to a person, much less an audience. I was ready to toss it all, but that drive to give back to all those who have believed in me, to properly thank mentors and experts alike who have helped me so much? To reach out, egoless, and make an impact? I continued to stretch myself and learned not only how to tell a story from the stage, but how to effectively lead from the stage. Not sell. Not close. My business doesn't require a hard sell; it's about creating connections between individuals.

Since supporting others in their own journey is so important to my own, speaking has come to play a pivotal role. I have been to countless trade shows and events for my company, A-List Connection, and each one has helped me build on those relationships. Years ago, as a member of the Silicon Valley Capital Club, I was handling one of my trade tables for an upcoming event and during the course of the day, amid the steady flow of traffic to the table, I was asked if I'd like to speak to a group of baby boomers at the Santa Clara Convention Center the next month. Stealing a page from Loral Langemeier, I said Yes! ... and then set about figuring out how.

I outlined my talk, had an amazing series of notes, rewrote my staffing schedule to cover the table, and I was ready to knock it out of the park.

Somewhere between home and the SVCC, and I'm not sure where, I picked up a hitchhiker. I bet you know him. Murphy? Yep. As I was checking in to get ready to take the stage, I was informed that my time was now doubled since another speaker had cancelled, and my notes were … right on the kitchen counter where I'd placed them so I could remember them. Since I'd passed out a worksheet for the audience, I also realized that they were more engaged with it that with me. An audience filled with the tops of heads, not faces. To add insult to injury, the podium had apparently been set up for Michael Jordan, so if I craned my neck, my little 5'4" head just *might* be visible. I could see Tragedy waiting in the wings of the stage, ready to swoop in after I burst into flames. Something funny happened, though.

Phil Donahue rescued me.

I took a deep breath. I picked out a couple of friendly looking tops of heads in the crowd. I decided that I was going to make it – I was going to wing it – but I was going to make it. I pulled a page from The Donahue Show and got off the stage and into the audience; and I started to talk. Just having a conversation with these folks. They had come to hear tips and options for singles in the "over 40" crowd, and I gave them that and more. I went somewhere into a zone and just began giving. I knew the material like the back of my hand, and, much to the annoyance of the timekeeper, I quit watching their cues and promptly lost all track of time.

At some point, I noticed that the poor soul who was keeping time was jumping around like a toddler who needed to go to the bathroom, and I gave what may be the worst speech closing ever seen. "Yikes, I've gone over! If you'd like to connect with me, just stop by and see me at the back of the room." As I went to the back of the room, a member of the audience thanked me for the great talk and asked where I would be speaking next. I chuckled and said I had no idea - she asked me to speak to her group the next week! The ripple effect of speaking one-to-many had begun. There was a short break between speakers, and as I got organized back at my trade show table, a huge stream of listeners made their way back to speak with me. That day, I was able to share with those people my ideas and help them to see ways that they could positively impact their lives regardless of their relationship status. My goal had been to make a difference in one person's life; that and so much more happened, and since time is our most precious commodity, I saw how I could reach many people at once. It was a life-changing experience.

After that early awkward experience, I've had a flood of wonderful speaking offers. I choose where I speak based upon tangible results for the participants and ongoing support after. It's still more enjoyable to support other speakers and that same sentiment was echoed by my close friend Steve Sherzer shortly before he passed in 2010: "Who cares what others think, Sandra? Go help people support one another." In the end, he showed me that I simply needed to follow my passion now or I never would – and that passion for service to others is my guide on this journey.

The Speaker's Profitizer

How to Deliver Presentations That Maximize Your Impact & Your Income

Discover the secret formula for delivering presentations that engage and inspire your audience to take action.

- Frustrated with presentations that don't bring the results you wanted?
- Want your audience to take action and say "Yes" to working with you?
- Learn the perfect balance of delivering quality content and having them beg for more ... in a NON-SALESY way!

**GET THIS FREE PROVEN
PRESENTATION TEMPLATE NOW**

This Presentation Template Has Been Proven to Increase Sales by 100%

With
Nancy Matthews & Trish Carr

Go to:
SpeakingforFunandProfit.com

FREE Live Tele-class Every Wednesday!

Join WPN Founder, Nancy Matthews, and say goodbye to "Hump Day" and give every day that weekend feeling!

Our free weekly tele-class has been featuring top experts and trusted authorities since 2010 to keep you up to date and in the know for winning in business and in life.

Go to:
WomensProsperityNetwork.com/Wow

"The WPN Global community supports every aspect of my life! The mastermind workshops and conversations with the other women of WPN inspire me and encourage me to be the best "ME" I can be – a wife, a mother, a friend and a business woman. Thank you WPN. My life wouldn't be the same without you."

~ Vanessa McGovern

44142046R00110

Made in the USA
Charleston, SC
19 July 2015